THE
FEDERAL
REPUBLIC
OF
GERMANY

THE
FEDERAL
REPUBLIC
OF
GERMANY

A CONCISE HISTORY

Alfred Grosser

Translated by
Nelson Aldrich

FREDERICK A. PRAEGER, *Publishers*
New York · Washington · London

Frederick A. Praeger, *Publishers*
111 Fourth Avenue, New York 3, N.Y., U.S.A.
77–79 Charlotte Street, London W.1, England

Published in the United States of America in 1964
by Frederick A. Praeger, Inc., Publishers

Fourth printing, 1966

First published in France in 1963 by Presses Universitaires de
France in the "Collection Que Sais-je?" under the title
La République Fédérale d'Allemagne

Library of Congress Catalog Card Number: 64-16677

Printed in the United States of America

Contents

THE
FEDERAL
REPUBLIC
OF
GERMANY

I

Occupied Germany

THE German Federal Republic was born in 1949; Hitler's Third Reich had collapsed in 1945. This four-year interval between two German governments probably did more to shape the face of Germany today than did the twelve years of National Socialist dictatorship or the fourteen years of the shaky Weimar Republic that preceded Hitler. Whether one considers the present international status of the country, its political institutions or ideological conflict, the consequences of those four years are today innumerable.

1. A Lost and Broken Germany

In the past, a conquered country usually experienced one of two fates: Either, by annexation, it simply ceased to exist as an independent state; or, it was forced to accept the conditions laid down by the conqueror but was allowed to keep a government of its own, if only to sign the peace treaty. At the end of World War II, the Allies chose a third solution: Germany would not disappear, the German nation would continue to exist; but the victorious powers

3

would assume the internal and external sovereignty of the defeated country. On June 5, 1945, the British, American, Soviet, and French governments announced that they were taking over supreme powers in Germany.

But *what* Germany? A second declaration of the same day—announcing the creation of four zones of occupation and the joint Four-Power administration of Berlin—referred to the German frontiers of December 31, 1937. These included the Saar (returned to Germany after a referendum in 1935, organized in conformity with the Versailles Treaty of 1919) but excluded all territory seized by Hitler. At the very moment that this declaration was issued, however, one-fifth of the territory thus defined had already been taken away from Germany at the direction of the Big Four. On April 21, the U.S.S.R. had handed over to Poland the administration of those regions lying to the east of a line marked by the Oder River and one of its tributaries, the Western Neisse—with the exception of a part of East Prussia which the Soviet Union administered directly. At Tehran in 1943 and at Yalta in February, 1945, Stalin, Roosevelt, and Churchill had long debated this problem of the western borders of Poland. The Potsdam Agreement of August 2, 1945, was to agree "in principle to the proposal of the Soviet Government concerning the ultimate transfer to the Soviet Union of the city of Königsberg and the area adjacent to it," and it recorded the agreement of the three chiefs of government "that, pending the final determination of Poland's western frontier, the former German territories . . . shall be placed under the administration of the Polish State, and for such purposes should not be considered as part of the Soviet Zone of occupation in Germany."

The division of Germany into zones of occupation had been arranged even before the cessation of hostilities. A protocol signed in London on September 12, 1944, provided for three zones. Greater Berlin, however, would be divided into three sectors of occupation to be administered jointly by the U.S.A., Britain, and the U.S.S.R. This protocol was spelled out in greater detail in two agreements signed, also in London, the following November. With the creation of a French occupation zone by an additional agreement on May 1, 1945, these texts defined in advance how the defeated nation would be administered. The day after the final victory, each of the signatories honored the agreements. On July 1, American troops drew back from those parts of Saxony and Thuringia which they had overrun in their advance, because the area was in the Soviet zone; in Greater Berlin, the three Western Allies moved into their occupation sectors following the capture of the city by the Red Army.

According to the Potsdam Agreement, "During the occupation period, Germany shall be treated as a single economic unit," and there was to be, "so far as is practicable, uniformity of treatment of the German population throughout Germany." In theory, supreme authority was vested in the Allied Control Council, meeting in Berlin. The Council was composed of the four commanders in chief (whose decisions had to be unanimous), assisted by political advisers and by specialized directorates corresponding to ministerial departments. France, however, was hostile to even the slightest suggestion of a unified state in Germany and cast its veto against setting up any centralized German authorities, even those that had been provided at Potsdam for Finance, Communications, and Foreign Trade. A true four-power management of Germany thus became technically unrealizable. Moreover, each commander in chief had, in a sense, a double personality: In Berlin, as a member of the Control Council, he shared with three others the problem of determining to what extent he, as absolute ruler of his zone, should carry out the decrees of the Council. But, since it is far easier to govern alone than to govern *à quatre*, none of the members was much disposed to grant the Control Council great authority. The zones, therefore, soon became rather like independent countries under separate foreign governments.

Thus, each of the Big Four interpreted in his own way the purposes of the occupation as these had been defined at Potsdam. They included denazification, demilitarization, and "development of local responsibility" in preparation for "the eventual reconstruction of [the German people's] life on a democratic and peaceful basis . . . [so that] it will be possible for them in due course to take their place among the free and peaceful peoples of the world."

2. *Physical and Moral Ruins*

Whatever the errors committed by the occupation forces, they had one major excuse: The land they had taken over was in utter chaos. For the first time since 1814, Germany had been devastated by war. But a war such as this, devastation such as this, would have been inconceivable in 1814. Not one major city had been spared the terrible bombardments for which the German *Luftwaffe* had itself given the cue in Coventry and Rotterdam. The fighting on land and Hitler's scorched-earth policy had completed the destruction. By the end of the war, few Germans were still living in their homes. Millions of city-dwellers sought refuge in the countryside, and millions of others had fled westward before the advancing tide of the Red Army. Every German male, including fifteen-year-old boys, had been mobilized. Communications, food provisions, administration—all had ceased to exist. And into this chaos were thrown additional millions of Germans from the countries of Central Europe and the territories beyond the Oder-Neisse.

According to the Potsdam Agreement, "The three Governments . . . recognize that the transfer to Germany of German populations . . . in Poland, Czechoslovakia and Hungary will have to be undertaken. They agree that any transfers that take place should be effected in an orderly and humane manner." But "in Poland" meant to the Poles and Russians that it was also going to be necessary to expel the inhabitants of the regions to the east of the Oder-Neisse line. In a strict reading of the agreement, this interpretation is difficult to justify, but it is not far from Churchill's original proposals. In any event, the massive expulsion of populations generally took place under the most appalling conditions. Hundreds of thousands of old men, children, and women never arrived at their intended destination.

This misery was the consequence of the concept of "total war" that Hitler had chosen to apply. The peoples he attacked had suffered terribly before his regime collapsed in total defeat. In theory, at least, there was no desire for vengeance: The entire German people were indicted to determine the measure of their guilt. In practice, however, the weight of suffering on both sides was too great for equity and calm to prevail. The sweeping generalizations of the victors were understandable, but they shocked and wounded millions of individuals, each of whom had suffered a personal tragedy of his own. The policies of denazification and demilitarization, in short, were applied to a wretched and demoralized people. At the end of 1946, 100,000 people were dying of hunger in the city of Hamburg alone. In Cologne, only 12 per cent of the children were of normal weight. How could one speak of morality to a people who were just managing to keep alive by expedients beyond all morality?

And yet, the occupying powers were right in wishing to punish those Germans who were guilty, to eliminate Nazism, and to purge the country of all it had stood for. To do this, it was necessary to begin with a clear and indisputable definition of guilt and of the phenomenon of National Socialism. From November 20, 1945, to October 1, 1946, the surviving leaders of the Third Reich were brought to trial at Nuremberg. They were accused of three orders of crime: "crimes against peace," "war crimes," and "crimes against humanity." The latter were specified as "including but not limited to murder, extermination, enslavement, deportation, imprisonment, torture, rape or other inhumane acts committed against any civilian population, or persecutions on political, racial, or religious grounds whether or not in violation of the domestic laws of the country where perpetrated." The basic justification for the twelve death penalties handed down by the court lay in the necessity of punishing those responsible for a barbarism without precedent in history. But the weakness of the Nuremberg Trials lay in the fact that no action was taken against the crimes committed, either before or after the trial, in the name of the victorious powers, and in the fact that only the Allies appointed the members of the court, whose impartiality should have been beyond all suspicion.

Although to punish the war criminals was a relatively simple matter, the problem of "the duty to disobey" was never discussed in any depth by the international military tribunal. But how did one judge indirect guilt? How could German life be "purified"? An appreciable number of Germans themselves recognized the problem and in 1945 did not hesitate to declare openly that they had been guilty of weakness and cowardice. At the same time, they tried to persuade as many of their compatriots as possible to examine their own consciences: In the writings of this period, few words crop up as often as *Besinnung*—turning back on oneself. This kind of moral guilt was not measurable by judicial norms, but it was precisely what the occupying powers failed to understand as they carried out their denazification program. That program was administered according to a number of successive provisions that were often contradictory. For instance, only individual cases were considered—and quite rightly so, since the notion of collective guilt had not been written into the texts; instead of taking up the most important of these, however, the entire population had to be sifted through; in the American zone alone, the authorities soon found themselves faced with some 13 million dossiers. Moreover, the decisive criterion for guilt was membership in the Nazi Party and its numerous appendages —political, paramilitary, athletic, or cultural. But membership in an organization should not have been absolute proof of Nazism, above all in the bureaucracy, whereas many of those who most actively supported the regime never belonged to the Party.

Then, too, there was outright injustice in that the cam-

paign of purification was more or less severe in proportion
as the Germans concerned were more or less useful to the
occupying powers. The spiritual future of the country
doubtless called for a purge of the educational system, but
the guilt of many a great industrialist, administrator, or
judge certainly exceeded that of the pathetic schoolteachers
or bureaucrats who were purged during the occupation.
The authorities exempted only the most powerful of the
Nazi collaborators, and often failed even to question them
too closely, under the pretext that their support of the Nazi
regime had been "technical" and not political, and by
invoking the (often real) need for their services to bring
the country out of chaos. Soon, of course, the East-West
conflict was to enlarge the number of Hitler's faithful who
would henceforth be considered indispensable.

The occupying authorities committed still other errors,
and they did not always set the Germans a good example of
that liberal democracy which in theory they claimed to
uphold. At the same time, however, they accomplished a
considerable job of reconstruction. Little by little, political
life re-emerged in Germany. The men whom the Allies
placed in power showed themselves to be so competent
that, when the time came, they were to become the elected
political elite of the Federal Republic. Beginning in 1945,
the French military government encouraged contacts between the young people of France and Germany, and from
these contacts was born a working cooperation the forma-
tive effects of which cannot be overestimated. In the economic field, the three Western powers adopted on June 18,
1948, a decisive and drastic monetary reform, which had
spectacular results in spurring a vigorous "take-off" of the
German economy. But already, by that date, such a reform

must be understood as a symptom of the growing division of Germany.

3. Divided Allies, Divided Germany

By October, 1945, it was apparent that the differences between the major powers were becoming almost insurmountable. At issue were problems that had nothing to do with Germany, as well as those posed by the occupation. For a whole series of reasons, the Control Council made hardly any more decisions after the month of March, 1946, and this naturally changed the way one could speak of "German unity." While in the Four-Power talks of April–May and June–July, 1946, and of March–April and November, 1947, the economic unity and central administration of Germany were still discussed in the terms of the Potsdam Agreement, there was a progressive fusion, from 1946 to 1949, of the three Western zones. This came about for two very different reasons: First, economic efficiency required the abolition of the customs barriers between the zones; and, second, the steadily worsening relations between East and West led both sides to regard Germany no longer as an enemy to be carefully watched or a defeated aggressor to be punished, but as a pawn in the new rivalry and soon a potential partner in the Cold War. Taken together, these two factors led Great Britain and the U.S.A. to grant increasing responsibilities to the Germans, first of all in the economic field. The U.S.S.R. did the same on its side, while France held aloof until the moment when her world policies finally took precedence over her one-sided concern with Germany.

From 1946 on, therefore, the process would be this: The

greater the tension between the two blocs, the more authority would be handed over by each side to "its" Germany,
but also the more profound the rupture would be between
those two Germanies. The birth of two German governments in 1949 did little to halt this chain of events. Moreover, a heavy mortgage was henceforth riding on West
German foreign policy, inasmuch as the German Federal
Republic would have, so to speak, a built-in stake in the
growing international tension as a reinforcement of its own
position.

On May 25, 1947, the first German Economic Council
was created for the combined British and American zones.
On July 12, representatives of the sixteen countries accept-
ing American aid declared in Paris that "the German economy must be integrated into the economy of Europe."
Eventually, West Germany would be a member of the
Organization of European Economic Cooperation, though
at first it would be represented by the three military governors. In the East, the German People's Congress met for the
first time on December 6, 1947. And, in the West, on February 9, 1948, the Frankfort Charter was published, estab-
lishing for the Anglo-American zone a sort of economic
government consisting of an executive branch and a legislature. On March 10, the East German Economic Commission
was granted broader powers, and on March 19, the Russian
general Sokolovsky made a spectacular exit from the Allied
Control Council in Berlin, thus ending the meetings of that
authority.

But it was the month of June, 1948, that saw the out-
break of one of the most serious crises of the postwar
period. On June 4, the results were published of a conference held in London between representatives of Great

Britain, France, and the Benelux countries. The signatories declared their intention of setting up an international authority of the Ruhr and charged the military governors of Germany with the task of preparing, in cooperation with local authorities, to convoke a constituent assembly for all West Germany. Two weeks later came the monetary reform referred to above. East Germany replied with a monetary reform of its own on June 23 and applied it equally to the whole of Greater Berlin. From this resulted the breakdown of the Kommandatura, the rise of a municipality of East Berlin, and the dramatic Berlin blockade, which was to continue until the Four-Power Accord of May 5, 1949.

At the beginning of April, 1949, a series of agreements was signed in Washington that fused the French zone with the already combined American and British zones and created an Allied High Commission that would replace the military governments as soon as West Germany had its own government. On May 8, the Constituent Parliamentary Council at Bonn adopted the Basic Law (*Grundgesetz*) of the future Federal Republic of Germany. The three Western Allies, however, vetoed the proposal to include West Berlin in the new state. In the Russian zone on May 15, elections were held for the Third People's Congress, and, fifteen days later, that body adopted a constitution for the Democratic Republic of Germany. In West Germany, the first elections were held on August 16, 1949, and by September, the institutions of the Federal Republic were complete. Theodor Heuss was elected President, and he proposed Dr. Konrad Adenauer, the head of the largest party, as Chancellor.

II

The Foundations of the
New State

THE new state of West Germany was born in 1949
under difficult circumstances. Its sovereignty was at
first greatly restricted, and though it would slowly be
established more firmly, it would still remain limited. At
the same time, the Federal Republic represented the first
German democracy the legitimacy of which was not challenged by its citizens and in which respected judges could
establish the superiority of law over arbitrary will, even if
it were the will of the political majority.

1. The Basic Law

The Occupation Statute, which went into effect at the
same time as the Basic Law, began with these words, "In
the exercise of the supreme authority which is retained by
the Governments of France, the United States, and the
United Kingdom. . . ." It specified further that "the Federal State and the participating Länder shall have, subject
only to the limitations in this Instrument, full legislative,
executive and judicial powers." These limitations, however,

were substantial, concerning as they did disarmament and demilitarization, the control of the Ruhr, foreign affairs, respect for the Basic Law and the constitutions of the *Länder*, control over foreign trade and exchange—all of these theoretically remaining in the hands of the occupying powers. It was not until March 6, 1951, that the so-called "little revision" of the Statute permitted the creation of a German Ministry of Foreign Affairs, and even then it was heavily shackled. In practice, however, for a whole host of reasons—not the least being the skill of Konrad Adenauer, who became his own foreign minister—these texts were never strictly enforced. Moreover, as foreign minister, Adenauer was in a position to persuade his French, English, and American counterparts to give instructions to their High Commissioners in Germany not to bother the Chancellor. Legally, however, the Statute of 1949, as amended in 1951, remained enforceable until the agreements signed in Paris on October 23, 1954, went into effect in May of the following year. These read, in part:

> At the time when the present Convention comes into force, the Governments of France, the United Kingdom, and the United States of America will end their occupation of the Federal Republic, abrogate the Occupation Statute, and dissolve the Allied High Commission and the *Land* Commissariats in the Federal Republic.
>
> The Federal Republic will consequently exercise the full authority of a sovereign State in all internal and foreign affairs.

But, immediately afterward:

> In consideration of the international situation, which has until now prevented the reunification of Germany and the

conclusion of a peace treaty, the Three Powers reserve the rights and responsibilities previously exercised or reserved by them concerning Berlin and matters involving all Germany, including the reunification of Germany and a final peace settlement.

The way the Basic Law came into existence, though it mentioned the occupation in only the vaguest terms, clearly reflected the primacy of the occupying powers. Before it could be submitted to the German voters, it had to be approved by the military governors—a requirement that occasioned interminable discussions between the latter and the German lawmakers. Even the final letter of approval sent to Adenauer, then President of the Constituent Parliamentary Council, on May 12, 1949, contained reminders that the Basic Law was subordinate to the Occupation Statute and that the Allies were continuing to veto the inclusion of West Berlin in the Federal Republic.

Ratified by all the elected legislatures of the *Länder*, with the exception of the Bavarian Diet, the *Grundgesetz* provided the legal foundations for a state that declared itself to be sovereign and independent, but also transitional and divided:

> The German People in the *Länder* of Baden, Bavaria, Bremen, Hamburg, Hesse, Lower Saxony, North Rhine–Westphalia, Rhineland-Palatinate, Schleswig-Holstein, Württemberg-Baden, and Württemberg-Hohenzollern,
>
> CONSCIOUS of its responsibility before God and Men,
>
> ANIMATED by the resolve to preserve its national and political unity and to serve the peace of the world as an equal partner in a unified Europe,
>
> DESIRING to give a new order to political life for a transitional period,

HAS ENACTED, by virtue of its constituent power, this Basic Law of the Federal Republic of Germany. It has also acted on behalf of those Germans to whom participation was denied.

The entire German people is called on to achieve by free self-determination the unity and freedom of Germany....

This Basic Law shall cease to be in force on the day on which a constitution adopted by a free decision of the German people comes into force.

In 1919, the Constitutional Assembly of Weimar, which had been elected by universal suffrage, had been able to accomplish its work without foreign interference. The text it adopted was a true and definitive constitution, and the victorious powers of *that* war applied only the fewest and most temporary checks on the Weimar Republic's complete sovereignty and independence. Yet, by a seemingly astonishing paradox, the legitimacy of the Weimar regime was continually challenged by an ever-growing sector of German opinion, whereas the provisional and unfinished Federal Republic now enjoys a quiet stability that makes it rather similar to England and Sweden. There are differences of opinion in West German politics, but no party of any importance questions the regime itself.

There are two explanations for this: On the one hand, the Federal Republic profited from an exceptionally lucky circumstance, which equally benefited its first Chancellor and the winning party in the first elections. In 1919, it had seemed to many Germans that the Weimar Republic and its leaders were responsible for the catastrophic situation in which their defeated country found itself. But the worst moments in all German history occurred between 1944 and 1948, that is, under Hitler and the occupation. For the state created in 1949, its early years of growth and development coincided with the beginnings of an economic renaissance and a relatively rapid restoration of German prestige in the world. The words "republic" and "democracy," which after 1920 had been synonymous with humiliation and poverty, were, after 1950, if not synonymous at least contemporaneous with "escape from chaos" and "diplomatic and economic recovery." The regime was thereby strengthened, legitimized.

The Germany of the Weimar Republic, on the other hand, had been ideologically torn apart. On the extreme left, a Communist Party, which ultimately attained 17 per cent of the vote in November, 1932, had called for revolution, while to the right and extreme right, never a majority but always powerful even before Hitler's rise to power, devotion to the nation always went before devotion to democracy. The Federal Republic has not known these problems. Apart from what the country owes to its institutions and leaders, it is doubtless due to its international situation that West Germany enjoys an interior tranquility which its neighbor France, for example, has not known since 1947. For the Bonn government has been free of those attacks on legitimacy which are born of the throes of decolonization, and free of that unshakeably determined opposition which is entailed by the presence of a strong Communist Party in the period of the cold war. With no colonies, and almost unanimously anti-Communist—to the point of preferring to keep the nation divided rather than accept any form of reunification that would imply a rise of Communist influence—the Federal Republic has so far been able to make its institutions function on a basis of ideological consensus that is most propitious for the normal life of a pluralist democracy.

2. *Respect for the Constitution*

In general, a constitution takes its form in reaction to the nature of the regime that preceded it. The men charged with drawing up a constitution in Bonn gave much thought to the Weimar Republic when they argued the merits of such and such a clause. But, above all, they wished to register their profound disapproval of the Third Reich and their loyalty to the values that National Socialism had tried to destroy.

Whereas in the Weimar Constitution, a Bill of Rights (*Grundrechte*) occupied only second place—and even there, closely associated with a sort of "Bill of Duties"— in the Basic Law, the rights of men are listed at the outset of the document. Not simply a preamble announcing a number of guiding principles, as in the French constitutions of 1946 and 1958, the first article of the Basic Law's *Grundrechte* stipulates: "The following basic rights bind the legislature, the executive, and the judiciary as directly enforceable law." The break with the Hitlerian past appears clearly in wording such as: "The dignity of man is inviolable," and "No one may be prejudiced or favored because of . . . his parentage, his race . . . his homeland, his origin." Hitler had deprived immigrants and members of the opposition of their German nationality. Therefore, the Basic Law declares that a disqualification from German nationality is impossible if this results in statelessness. Over and above freedom of opinion, the rights of conscientious objectors are expressly guaranteed. They may be obliged to serve as replacements in the civil service, but their employment must not have the slightest connection with the armed forces. All the "classic" freedoms are, of course, guaranteed as well: freedom of association and assembly, freedom of expression, privacy in the mails, and the inviolability of the home.

The memory of the years 1929–33, however, did bring about the insertion of Article 18, which declared that anyone who misuses his rights to subvert freedom and democracy thereby forfeits those rights. The interpretation of such a provision is a delicate matter indeed, demanding the existence of a judiciary completely independent of political pressures as a guarantee against repressive action by the government. And the Federal Constitutional Court alone has the power to decide whether someone should be deprived of his rights.

The Court at Karlsruhe occupies an eminent place in the political system of the Federal Republic. The first reason for this is that, again in contrast to Hitler's dictatorship, legality passes in West Germany for a supreme value. The idea of a *Rechtsstaat* (a state founded on law) is manifested by both the representativity of the judiciary and by the authority of the Basic Law over the will of the majority.

The French people, for example, according to the Constitution of 1946, exercised their sovereignty "in constitutional issues by the votes of their representatives and by referendum. On all other issues . . . by their deputies in the National Assembly." Since 1958, their sovereignty is exercised "through their representatives and by way of referendum." In contrast, Article 20 of the Basic Law specifies that the German people themselves hold sovereignty "by separate legislative, executive, and judicial organs." Even if one believes that Montesquieu's theory of the division of powers no longer corresponds to the reality of contemporary political societies and that the three branches of government cannot be so nicely separated, one must still try to understand the full scope of this will to consider the judge as much a qualified representative of the people as the political leader. It had not been forgotten that on the day after the massacre of June 30, 1934, the most renowned German jurist had written: "The true Führer is always at the same time the true Judge. . . . The action of the Führer cannot be submitted to the bar of Justice; it is in itself the highest form of Justice."

A constitution may be of two completely different kinds. In France, for instance, it has for a long time been thought of as a technique—as a means of fixing the rules of the political game. It enables the political system to function, and that system is in any case founded on the will of the majority. Article 91 of the Constitution of 1946 had said: "The Constitutional Committee will study whether the laws passed by the National Assembly imply a revision of the Constitution." As recently as November 6, 1962, the Constitutional Council of the Fifth Republic declared itself incompetent to pronounce on laws "which, adopted by the people by referendum, constitute a direct expression of the national sovereignty." In both instances, the superiority of majority will over constitutional text is clearly affirmed. In the United States, on the other hand, the Constitution is an almost sacred charter, a basic law in the fullest sense. And the expression used by the German Parliamentary Council shows that they were mindful of the American example. Respect for the Basic Law must be so thoroughly imposed on all parts of government that the Chief of State himself will be its servant and not its protector. The Judiciary will fill that office of guardian—its role being therefore not simply to pronounce on the existing law. When the American Supreme Court rules on the issue of segregation, when the Court at Karlsruhe pronounces on the definition of freedom of information, it is not merely a question of a juridical interpretation of the Constitution, it is a matter of laying down and making explicit the moral values to which the national conscience bears witness.

The Federal Constitutional Court, the *Bundesverfassungs-gericht,** therefore passes long and well considered judgment. On January 17, 1957, for example, it declared null and void an article of the income-tax law that would have obliged married couples to declare a joint income and which, under a progressive tax, would have heavily penalized marriage in relation to, say, a system of concubinage. To the Federal Constitutional Court, this situation would have created a permanent violation of Article 6 of the Basic Law, which imposes on the state the obligation to protect the family and the married estate. The provision was thus annulled. Another example: Article 131 of the Basic Law obliges the federal legislators to regulate the legal status of all those, including refugees and political exiles, who "on May 8, 1945, were employed in the public service, have left the service for reasons other than those arising from civil service regulations or collective agreement rules, and have not until now been employed or are employed in a position not corresponding to their former one." A law

* Not to be confused with the Supreme Federal Court, the *Bundesgerichtshof,* also in Karlsruhe, which serves both as a highest court of appeal and, in cases concerning treason, as a court of the first instance.

of May 11, 1951, the so-called Law 131, set off a number of appeals to the Court at Karlsruhe from civil servants who felt their fundamental rights were being violated by numerous provisions in this law, but the tribunal dismissed the plaintiffs' cases. In doing so, it traced a grim picture of just what the civil service had been like under the Nazi regime and came to the following conclusion: It was in 1933 that the nature of the ties between the state and its employees underwent a complete change; it was in 1933 that the notion of acquired rights completely changed in meaning. The Court's judgment, of December 17, 1953, has constituted a veritable lesson on the nature of National Socialism, and a kind of negative definition of the function of a civil service in a pluralistic democracy.

The Court ruled against the government when, on February 28, 1961, it found that the creation of a second television network violated Article 5 of the Basic Law (freedom of opinion and of the press and mass media). For, although West German radio and television are organizations held in trust for the people and administered by representatives of the different political and social forces, the new network would have permitted the government direct control over broadcasting. And it ruled against the opposition Social Democrats—who then controlled the *Länder* governments of Hesse, Bremen, and Hamburg—when, in August, 1958, it declared unconstitutional the organization of referendums on the question of atomic armaments, on the grounds that a party may not misuse regional institutions to try to attain a national objective. The Court ruled in favor of the National Assembly, the defendant, and against two small political parties when, in January, 1957, it upheld the constitutionality of the restrictive clauses of the electoral law on elections to the federal legislature.* But, on many occasions, it has also annulled clauses in municipal electoral laws on the grounds that they penalized the candidates of purely local interests in favor of the parties. After having banned the Communist Party in 1956, the Court five years later declared unconstitutional an additional paragraph of the penal code (thereby annulling several judicial decisions by lower courts): The members and leaders of a prohibited party must not be prosecuted *a posteriori* for their membership in or services to the Party before its prohibition.

Even if some decisions of the Court may seem contestable, even if there exists in West Germany a danger similar to one that has sometimes been pointed out in America—that of a "government by judges"—the *Bundesverfassungsgericht* nevertheless is, in fact and in deed, the most significant of the institutions of the Federal Republic.

* See Chapter 4.

III

Political Institutions

THOUGH to a Frenchman it seems hardly centralized and to an American hardly federal, the German Federal Republic has, in its first fourteen years of existence, appeared to operate without a hitch. The domination of the cabinet over the parliament, perfectly understandable as it is in terms of both men and constitutions, is not, however, in any way a characteristic peculiar to the German parliamentary system. The decline of parliament is common to all European countries.

1. A Federal Republic

In 1949, when the *Bund* was formed, the *Länder* found themselves in a position of simultaneous power and weakness in relation to the federal government. They had been created before the *Bund*. Some of them, like Bavaria and Hesse in 1946, or Bremen and the Rhine–Palatinate in 1947, had already drawn up constitutions. The Constituent Parliamentary Council in Bonn had grown out of the *Landtage*. The Allies (and above all the French, who had a tendency to see in a centralized state the source of all

German evils) insisted on limiting the powers of the *Bund*. But, at the same time, the crushing tasks of reconstruction and of integrating the refugees could hardly be carried out piecemeal; they demanded, in fact, strong central direction. Moreover, the Federal Republic in 1949 faced what seemed then to be a fundamental structural problem: the lack of any ethnic, historical, or cultural unity in many of the "lands" it was supposed to federate. In dividing Germany into *Länder* after 1945, the Allies had not paid as much attention to German traditions as to the lines of the occupation zones. Bremen, for example, was made a *Land* simply because the Americans needed a free port in the British zone; the line separating the French and American zones cut Baden, Württemberg, and Hesse in two; and the Rhineland was divided between the French and British. As a result, the demarcations of the *Länder* were laid down along rather eccentric lines. Moreover, the influx of refugees from the East and the displacement of many thousands of Germans from one region to another during the war largely destroyed the ethnic unity of Bavaria and Württemberg.

Yet, though numerous plans to redraw the territorial lines were made, only one important modification occurred: As stipulated in Article 118 of the Basic Law, the three *Länder* of the Southwest—Württemberg-Baden, Württemberg-Hohenzollern, and Süd-Baden—fused in 1951 to form Baden-Württemberg, which reduced the number of *Länder* from eleven to nine. There have been ten since the political union of the Saar with the Federal Republic, which occurred on January 1, 1957. Then there is the case of West Berlin. According to Article 1 of the Berlin Constitution of September 1, 1950:

SECTION 1. Berlin is a German *Land* and at the same time a city;

2. Berlin is a *Land* of the German Federal Republic;

3. The Basic Law and the laws of the German Federal Republic are applicable to Berlin.

However, the veto of the occupying powers against Sections 2 and 3 forced the Berlin authorities to forego their application. Under Allied pressure, the Parliamentary Council had to agree that Berlin would not participate in the federal elections, that although the Berlin House of Representatives would send deputies to Bonn, and although the deputies would be seated in the *Bundestag*, they would have no voting rights. Yet the nature of Berlin as the true capital of Germany has always been asserted by West Germany, and West Berlin has become more and more assimilated into the Federal Republic as a *Land*. If the Berlin representatives at Bonn do not actually vote on the laws, they nevertheless take an active part in all debates, and participate in committee votes. In Berlin itself, moreover, the application of federal laws is accomplished in ever more simplified fashion. Today, the Mayor of Berlin generally simply promulgates the laws passed in Bonn without the intervention of the Berlin legislature.

In the whole of West Germany, there are nearly two thousand deputies and more than a hundred ministers in office at a given time. The most diverse government coalitions exist, or have existed, in the capitals of the *Länder*. Though often sluggish, political life on the level of the *Land* is still of very real importance. The general principles governing the respective powers of the *Bund* and the *Länder* are defined as follows in the Basic Law:

ARTICLE 30. The exercise of governmental powers and the discharge of governmental functions is incumbent on the *Länder* insofar as this Basic Law does not otherwise prescribe or permit.

ARTICLE 31. Federal law overrides *Land* law.

The Constitution gives to the *Bund* exclusive power in eleven areas, of which the most important are foreign affairs, questions of nationality, federal railroads and airways, currency and tariffs, postal and telephone communications, the creation of a Federal Office of Criminal Investigation, and Interpol. In twenty-three other matters, "the *Länder* have authority to legislate as long as, and to the extent that, the *Bund* does not use its legislative power." But these are important areas indeed: civil law, criminal law, organization of the judiciary, family status, the rights of association and assembly, refugees and displaced persons, war damages and reparations, economic legislation and work laws, the development of scientific research, nationalization, and "prevention of the abuse of economic power [antitrust laws]."

In cultural affairs and in education, the autonomy of the *Länder* is absolute. There is no federal Ministry of Education. The only instances of cooperation among the *Länder* are the Conference of Ministers of Education—merely a secretariat with no real powers—and, on the university level, the Conference of Rectors, which meets quite frequently and sometimes makes important decisions. That the religious organization of the schools varies completely from one *Land* to the next may seem only normal and even healthy, given the regional differences in matters of religion; but many Germans complain of the *Länder*'s incomprehension of the need for the country's intellectual, scientific, and artistic development to be fostered as a whole.

It is true, of course, that inequalities of wealth among the *Länder* create unequal opportunities for action. However, the system of state revenues is so organized as to go some way toward an equalization among the *Länder* according to need. Thus, while the resources of Schleswig-Holstein stood at 66 per cent of the average in 1961, those of North Rhine-Westphalia were at 114 per cent; but the system of equalization brought the figures to 86 per cent and 106 per cent. The division of tax revenues between the *Bund* and the *Länder* is extremely complex. The *Länder* turn over to the *Bund* 35 per cent of their taxes on income and corporations and retain the entire revenue from taxes on capital, inheritance, and automobiles. The *Bund* keeps all revenue from taxes on the consumer and on business turnover, as well as tariff revenue. One of the major political issues of 1963 was once again precisely this financial agreement between the *Bund* and the *Länder*.

2. Presidents of the Republic

The organs of the federal government have their seat in Bonn, a small city on the Rhine, which was chosen over Frankfort by the slimmest of margins on November 3, 1949. Aside from other arguments that were weighed in the decision, the most important factor in the choice of Bonn— situated as it is on the periphery of Germany's major lines of communication and poorly provided with the basic facilities for a capital—was its very inadequacy. How better to underline the provisional character of the Federal Republic? Frankfort could pass for a true capital, but this was a right that belonged to Berlin alone.

On the political level as in the legislative domain, the

division of power between the four central organs of government established by the Basic Law is clear enough in the texts but more difficult to grasp in practice. Members of the *Bundestag* are elected directly through universal suffrage. The federal government depends on a vote of investiture by the *Bundestag* and on prior designation by the President of the Republic. The second legislative assembly, the *Bundesrat,* represents the executive powers of the *Länder*. The President of the Republic is elected by a special Federal Convention including all members of the *Bundestag* and an equal number of delegates from the *Landtage*. His powers are very limited.

For the authors of the Basic Law, the problem was to annihilate all traces of the two factors that had given such great power to the presidents of the Weimar Republic, Ebert and Hindenburg: namely, direct election by universal suffrage and the power to make and unmake the heads of government, two aspects of presidential power that were added to by the incumbent's recourse to the limitless possibilities of power "in a state of emergency." Elected for five years (which, though two years less than in the time of Weimar, is still one year more than a legislative term), the President of the Federal Republic is eligible for only two successive terms of office. Moreover, the President's authority is far more limited than that of a president of the Fourth Republic in France, not to mention that of the Fifth. He does not preside over the cabinet, and, indeed, once a government is installed, he has no further constitutional contact with it except for the pure formalities of signing and countersigning laws. He designates the Chancellor but in certain cases the *Bundestag* can overrule him. The only two substantial powers he has are, in fact, the limited right of dissolution of the legislature and an opportunity to influence personally the course of policy quite outside any constitutional channels.

Dr. Theodor Heuss, the first President of the Republic, was elected on the second ballot in 1949, and in July, 1954, he was re-elected by a vote of 871 out of 987 votes cast. During his ten years in office, Dr. Heuss strongly affected what one may call the political tone, or style, of the German Federal Republic. His distaste for false pathos and decorum, his simplicity, and the sincerity of his democratic spirit combined to stamp the office of the supreme magistrate with a completely *civilian* character. This intellectual —a professor of modern history and political science who was at the same time a writer and politician—became so popular a figure in Germany that, after his retirement, one had the impression there were *two* presidents in Germany, especially since his successor was little known in 1959 and had been elected in rather unpleasant circumstances. (His death, in December, 1963, provoked a genuine and deep mourning throughout the country.) For, from February to June, 1959, Chancellor Adenauer had maneuvered the election in such a complicated and free-handed way that, quite apart from causing a sharp decline in his own prestige, he very nearly ruined all the prestige and authority inherent in the office of the presidency itself.

To prevent Professor Ludwig Erhard, Minister of Economics, from succeeding him as Chancellor, Adenauer had first proposed that he become President of the Republic. On March 3, Erhard had refused. On April 7, by a decision that was as sudden as it was apparently inexplicable, Adenauer declared himself a candidate for the presidency. At the same time as he multiplied the number of his declarations on the political incapacity of his own minister, he went before the country on radio and television to say that the duties and powers of the president were in fact far greater than had generally been believed—which was rather insulting to Heuss. When he realized, however, that the Constitution does not permit a president to bar from the Chancellorship a candidate who is backed by a solid majority,* Adenauer announced that he no longer wished the presidency. This was on June 6; the election was to take place on July 1. The Christian Democrats had precious little time to find an acceptable candidate.

The Federal Minister of Agriculture, Dr. Heinrich Lübke, possessed few admirers but many friends and no enemies. He was not yet 65. In his youth, he had been active in agricultural organizations and in 1931-33, he had been a member of the *Landtag* of Prussia. Under Hitler, he had been imprisoned. After the war, he had resumed his political career in West Germany; he was elected first to the *Landtag* of Düsseldorf and had become the *Land's* Minister of Agriculture; he then was a member of the *Bundestag* and finally a federal minister. His election to the Presidency was easily secured on the second ballot, by 521 votes against 386 for the Social Democrat candidate, Professor Carlo Schmid, 99 for the Free Democrat candidate, and 22 abstentions. Since 1959, Lübke's prestige has grown steadily. In more than one respect, his case is similar to that of President René Coty in France: A man is chosen for his discretion and honor to put an end to a

---

* The *Bundestag* can refuse to elect the man the President has proposed as Chancellor, and can elect another candidate instead without the President's advice or consent. It would have been enough to elect Erhard had a few Christian Democrats abstained on the vote for Adenauer's candidate and then voted for Erhard on a subsequent ballot.

difficult situation, and becomes popular precisely because of that discretion and dignity. A man who takes his duties and responsibilities with great seriousness, Lübke often intervened, unspectacularly but effectively, during the last declining period of Chancellor Adenauer's rule, especially during the *Spiegel* affair of November, 1962. Like his predecessor, he has known how to give the Federal Republic a sort of respectability without stiffness which is one of its most attractive characteristics.

3. Adenauer's Cabinets

The men who devised West Germany's Basic Law wished to assure governmental stability and at the same time make of the Chief Executive a true representative of the national assembly. To prevent a recurrence of the situation of 1932, when mutually hostile blocs in the opposition could and did unite to bring down a government but not to create one, they elaborated a parliamentary mechanism known as "a vote of constructive non-confidence":

ARTICLE 67. 1) The *Bundestag* can express its lack of confidence in the Federal Chancellor only by electing a successor by the majority of its members and by requesting the Federal President to dismiss the Federal Chancellor. The Federal President must comply with the request and appoint the person elected.

This procedure has never been employed at the federal level. But in Düsseldorf, the capital of the *Land* of North Rhine-Westphalia, whose constitution contains an analogous provision, a government coalition of Christian Democrats and Free Democrats was overthrown in 1956 by a

Social-Democrat–Free-Democrat coalition in this way. In Bonn, however, Adenauer's permanence in power owed nothing whatever to Article 67.

As leader of the largest parliamentary party, Adenauer was elected Chancellor on September 15, 1949, by 202 votes out of 402, a slim margin. Further successes in the elections of 1953 and 1957, when the Christian Democrats gained an absolute majority both in the country as a whole and in the legislature, solidified Adenauer's power. (But, in 1961, a slight decline and the need of Free-Democrat support forced him into long negotiations with this small party in order to form his fourth government.) In the course of each legislature, some changes had to be made in the cabinets, above all in the years 1953–57—when new posts were created and both the Free Democrats and the All-German Bloc (a party of refugee Germans) underwent successive crises. Later, in November, 1962, the *Spiegel* affair also caused a significant shake-up in the cabinet. Nevertheless, one cannot say of West Germany as of the Fifth Republic in France that it has experienced "ministerial instability with a stable government." (*See Table 1.*)

In theory, the powers of the Chancellor are no greater than those of a head of government under the Fourth Republic. "He determines, and is responsible for, general policy," says Article 65, but "within the limits of this general policy, each Federal Minister conducts the business of his department autonomously and on his own responsibility. The Federal Government decides on differences of opinion between the Federal Ministers." How, then, did it come about that Konrad Adenauer exercised for so long an apparently sovereign power, to the point that some observers spoke of a *Kanzlerdemokratie?*

The cleverness, authority, and personal prestige of the man answer only part of the question. There are at least two other considerations. First, more than the Chancellor's personal tastes, the very nature of the problems facing West Germany from the outset placed primary importance on foreign policy. This factor tended to broaden the role of the head of government, all the more so in that Adenauer was his own Foreign Minister until 1955. Second, and most important, is the fact that Adenauer continuously filled two jobs at the same time: He was Chancellor and also president of the dominant political party.

By temperament even more than by circumstances, Adenauer always had a strong hold over his cabinet, to the point that no serious decision was ever taken in his absence. The vice-chancellorship of the government remained an office without any real power, whether it was held by Franz Blücher, who was in any case very discreet, or by the prestigious Economics Minister Ludwig Erhard, who was long the popular as well as the party choice to succeed Adenauer. When the Chancellor went on holiday, his actual replacement was for a long time Hans Globke, Director (*Ministerialdirektor*), then Secretary of State (*Staatssekretär*) in the Chancellery.

But while Globke never was more than an executor of the Chancellor's wishes, in the other ministries the *Staatssekretär* is often the true head of a department. Situated at the top of the professional administrative hierarchy, the secretary of state is in theory appointed at the discretion of the minister. In fact, the holders of these positions change only rarely. (In the *Spiegel* affair, the Christian Democrat secretary of state who failed to keep the Free Democrat Minister of Justice informed had been in office since 1949.

Table 1. Five Federal Cabinets

Principal Ministers*	First Cabinet (September, 1949)	Second Cabinet (October, 1953)	Third Cabinet (October, 1957)	Fourth Cabinet (November, 1961)	(December, 1962)	Fifth Cabinet (October, 1963)
Chancellor	Adenauer	Adenauer	Adenauer	Adenauer		Erhard
Vice-Chancellor	*Blücher*	*Blücher*	Erhard	Erhard		*Mende*
Foreign Affairs	Adenauer (post created, March, 1951)	Adenauer / Von Brentano (June, 1955)	Von Brentano	Schröder		Schröder
Interior	Heinemann / Lehr (October, 1950)	Schröder	Schröder	Höcherl		Höcherl
Justice	*Dehler*	*Neumeyer* / Von Merkatz (October, 1956)	Schäffer	*Stammberger*	*Bucher*	*Bucher*
Economy	Erhard	Erhard	Erhard	Erhard		Schmücker

Finance	Schäffer	Schäffer		Etzel	*Starke*	*Dahlgruen*	*Dahlgruen*
All-German Affairs	Kaiser	Kaiser		Lemmer	Lemmer	Barzel	*Mende*
Defense			Blank (post created, June, 1955) Strauss (October, 1956)	Strauss	Strauss	Von Hassel	Von Hassel

*Names of Free Democrat ministers are in italics. All others are C.D.U./C.S.U., except Von Merkatz, who moved from the German Party to the C.D.U. in 1960.

Party representation in each cabinet, including the Chancellor:

	C.D.U./C.S.U.	F.D.P.	D.P.	B.H.E.
1949 14 members	9	3	2	—
1953 19 members	11	4	2	2
1957 18 members	16	—	2	—
1961 21 members	16	5	—	—
1963 21 members	16	5	—	—

For this man, loyalty to his party and a sense of solidarity with other secretaries of state was above his loyalty to his immediate superior in the Ministry of Justice.)

Secretaries of state also have a tendency, like many Germans, to believe that the effective solutions to problems of statecraft are technical and not political, that politicians are unnecessary until the professional administrators have been shown to be powerless or ineffective. And it is an indisputable fact that more laws are submitted to, and passed by, the legislature on the initiative of the government than on the legislature's. This phenomenon, observable in all contemporary governments, is particularly obvious in the Federal Republic. (*See Table 2.*) The reasons for it are numerous—increasing centralization of the state and the growth of a corpus of federal law, the extreme complexity of the laws to be drawn upon and adopted, etc.—but it does help explain the domination of executive over legislative powers, as well as the feeling of frustration that can arise in a parliament dispossessed by both the government and the party bosses.

TABLE 2. ORIGIN OF LEGISLATIVE MEASURES

Legislative measures initiated by the	1949–53		1953–57		1957–61	
	Number introduced	Number passed	Number introduced	Number passed	Number introduced	Number passed
Government	472	392	446	368	401	348
Bundestag	301	141	414	132	207	74
Bundesrat	32	12	17	7	5	2

4. The Successor: Ludwig Erhard

The affair of the 1959 presidential election, the relative failure of the CDU in the 1961 elections, and its many following electoral defeats in the *Länder* all demonstrated that Konrad Adenauer's prestige—which had contributed so much to the victory of his party in 1957—was at a decidedly low ebb. Despite his age, however, the Chancellor had no desire whatever to relinquish his power. To those who urged him to quit, Adenauer would offer an argument that went something like this: "One can't very well leave after *these* elections, which did, after all, represent a victory for the CDU. We must wait at least two years. . . . What's more, one can't turn over the leadership in this struggle to a newcomer: He will need at least two years in which to familiarize himself with the job."

National elections in West Germany are held every four years. Adenauer's reasoning had been convincing between 1957 and 1961, but, in 1962, it was rejected, and the aging Chancellor was obliged to retire halfway between two general elections. On October 15, 1963, he handed in his resignation to the President of the Republic. He was then 87 years old and had been Chancellor for fourteen years. For the future of German democracy, it was a good thing that his departure had come after a period of relative decline in his popularity; for the succession was thereby accomplished with a minimum of difficulty. The irreplaceable man of providence had become quite replaceable.

In spite of Adenauer's overt hostility to him, no candidate for the Chancellorship could rival Ludwig Erhard. Even the reluctance of certain party leaders counted for nothing when weighed against the simple fact that, next to Adenauer, Erhard was the only man in the CDU who had a personal prestige and reputation among the electorate. It was not, then, the party that placed Erhard in the Chancellery, it was the public-opinion polls. The day after

Adenauer's resignation, he was elected Chancellor by 279 votes against 180, with 24 abstentions and one invalid ballot. Retaining most of his former associates in their posts, his principal changes were to bring Erich Mende, president of the Free Democratic Party, into the government as Vice-Chancellor and Minister for All-German Affairs, and to appoint Kurt Schmücker, until then president of the *Bundestag's* Economic Affairs Committee, to the Ministry of Economics. Another of his appointments was to prove more unfortunate. Hans Krüger, a deputy in the *Bundestag* since 1957 and since 1958 president of the powerful refugee roof organization, the *Bund der Vertriebenen, Vereinigten Landsmannschaften und Landesverbände,* was forced to resign on January 22, 1964, after having been relieved of his duties by the Chancellor. Evidence furnished by East German authorities proved that he had hidden an unsavory past as the presiding judge of a Nazi tribunal in Poland during the war. Politically, however, the most important change was the departure of Hans Globke as secretary of state in the Chancellery. The official reason given was that Globke had reached the retirement age of 65; yet it appears that his successor, Ludger Westrick, a loyal associate of Erhard (having been secretary of state in the Ministry of Economics since 1951), was born in 1894.

Abroad, in the United States as in France, people had become so used to identifying the Federal Republic with Konrad Adenauer that they did not even suspect that Ludwig Erhard had been playing an important role in West German public life even before the rebirth of the German state. In 1945, when the war was coming to a halt and Germany lay in ruins, Konrad Adenauer had been rein-installed by the Americans in his native province as mayor of Cologne in June. (This was the same post from which he had been driven by the Nazis in 1933 after sixteen years in office and from which the British would again expel him in October, 1945.) The next year, he was elected president of the new Christian Democratic Party in the British occupation zone; from 1948 to 1949, he was president of the parliamentary council that framed the Basic Law in Bonn. In short, Adenauer was used to being president of something: Even before 1933, he had presided over the Upper House of Prussia, of which the Rhineland was then a part.

In 1945, for his part, Ludwig Erhard had no political past. Born in Fürth, Bavaria, on February 4, 1897, he saw service in World War I after 1916, and was discharged in 1919 with the rank of sergeant, after being badly wounded at Ypres. A graduate of the Nuremberg *Handelshochschule*, a student of economics and sociology at Frankfort, he received his doctorate and abandoned private business for research. From 1928 to 1942, he was research assistant, assistant director, then director of an institute for economic research attached to the *Handelshochschule*. Pushed aside for his refusal to join the Nazi party, he became an economic consultant in private business and, after the German defeat, was called in by the Americans to reorganize the industry of the Fürth-Nuremberg region.

Then, on October 3, 1945, Erhard—still a "technocrat" without political affiliation—became Economics Minister in the second government of the *Land* of Bavaria. This was a coalition cabinet, presided over by a Social Democrat. Erhard did not retain his post in the next government, headed by a Christian Democrat, but in 1947, at the same time as he was made honorary professor of political economy at the University of Munich, he found himself upgraded from the Bavarian echelon to that of the combined British-American occupation zone, first as president of the Advisory Committee on Currency and Credit, then, in February, 1948, as director of the economic-affairs directorate created by the Frankfort Charter.

One of his first tasks was to put the finishing touches on the ways and means of the monetary reform—one of the rare Allied measures that escaped domestic German criticism, if not in its details at least in its underlying principle. Its palpable success seemed to be a sort of miracle. From one day to the next, the windows and counters of stores filled with goods, though in reality this was because the owners had previously kept their stocks out of sight while waiting for the return of a healthy currency. Soon thereafter, Erhard took on the responsibility for doing away with rationing, even though this meant running the risk of a sudden rise in prices and a return of scarcity. Neither occurred: Erhard had won a decisive victory. Thus, when he joined the CDU shortly before the legislative elections for the first *Bundestag* in 1949, Erhard brought to the party quite as much as he stood to gain from it. On the policy level, moreover, one can say that it was the CDU that joined Erhard, not Erhard the CDU. After the party's narrow victory, Adenauer scarcely hesitated before turning over the Ministry of Economics to the prophet of the *Soziale Marktwirtschaft*. For the next fourteen years, they would govern together. Apart from Erhard, only Hans-Christoph Seebohm, Minister of Transport, retained a position in all four Adenauer governments—he has also retained his portfolio in the Erhard cabinet.

Despite generally pessimistic auguries, the new Chancellor has enjoyed one success after another. In regional elections, the CDU has fared better and better at the polls; there have been successful mediations of social conflicts; Erhard has established cordial relations with President Johnson, General de Gaulle, and the British leaders. Finally, his relations with the Social Democrat opposition have been excellent, and he has demonstrated a sensitivity, a moderation, and a good will with respect to the parliament which was not among Konrad Adenauer's strong points.

5. Bundesrat *and* Bundestag

The *Bundesrat* is the linear descendant of the eighteenth-century *Reichstag*, the *Bundestag* of Frankfort (1815–66), Bismarck's *Bundesrat*, the *Reichsrat* of the Weimar Republic, and the Conference of Minister Presidents which met from 1947 to 1949. Article 50 of the Basic Law stipulates that, through the *Bundesrat*, "The *Länder* participate . . . in the legislation and administration of the *Bund*." Though it is a legislative assembly, it has nevertheless retained the essential characteristic of its predecessors, that of being composed of representatives of the executive branches of the *Länder:* "The *Bundesrat* consists of members of the *Länder* governments." If there is no strict numerical equality in the number of representatives from each *Länder*, as in the U.S. Senate, it is still true that the smaller *Länder* are greatly favored over the larger. Each *Land* has at least three votes; those having more than 2 million inhabitants have four votes; and those having more than 6 million inhabitants have five votes. (Table 3 shows the distribution.)

The *Bundesrat* has to a great extent become what the makers of the constitution wished—namely, the House of

TABLE 3. REPRESENTATION IN THE *Bundesrat*

Länder	Number of Delegates	Population (in millions) June, 1960
North Rhine-Westphalia	5	15.7
Bavaria	5	9.4
Baden-Württemberg	5	7.6
Lower Saxony	5	6.8
Hesse	4	6.8
Rhineland-Palatinate	4	4.7
Schleswig-Holstein	4	3.4
Hamburg	3	1.8
Saar	3	1.0
Bremen	3	0.7
Total	41	
West Berlin	4	2.2

the *Länder*, and an assembly of wise men counterbalancing the centralizing pull of the government and the tendency to demagoguery in the *Bundestag*. The major share of its work is done in committees. Each committee has one representative from each *Land*, who may be a high administrative officer. Any bill proposed either by the government or by the *Bundestag* goes to the competent committee for review. The opinion of the committee, often unanimous, is then submitted to the governments of the various *Länder*. And herein lies one of the great strengths of the *Bundesrat*, providing it with the leverage to participate fully in the administration of the Federal Republic, as had been stipulated in the Basic Law. For while the representatives in the *Bundestag* are often ill at ease when discussing technicalities with the government ministers, who enjoy access to all the classified information of their departments, the *Bundesrat*, supported by and representing the administrative know-how of the *Länder* governments, can stand up to the pressures put on the legislature by federal bureaucrats.

The legislative power of the *Bundesrat* depends on the nature of the bills it considers. In the case of a so-called federative law, for which its approval is necessary (*Zustimmungsgesetz*), its veto power is absolute. In other matters, the *Bundestag* may overcome the opposition of the *Bundesrat* by a qualified majority vote. Conflicts between the two houses are, however, rare, thanks to the efficient working of an organization known as the Conciliation Commission (*Vermittlungsausschuss*). Its twenty-two members, eleven from each house, are seated *à titre personnel* and are responsible to neither a parliamentary group nor a *Land* government. The Commission meets behind closed doors, far removed from the spotlight of publicity. By majority vote, its members determine the changes in a bill that they think will make it acceptable to both houses. The Commission has no powers of decision: the two Houses must vote on the modifications proposed. In general, it is the *Bundesrat* that most often appeals to the Commission. In the course of the first three legislatures, from 1949 to 1961, 181 bills were submitted to the Commission for mediation; of these, 177 were finally ratified by both houses in the form proposed by the Commission.

In 1949, the city of Bonn had no building, palace, or public building that could conceivably have served the needs of a parliament. It was necessary to build, and build fast. Very soon, there arose on the banks of the Rhine a white structure, modern but not aggressively so, to which new and taller wings are constantly being added. Though built outside the center of town, the Parliament is increasingly hemmed about by other buildings, many of which look rather like temporary barracks. The *Bundestag* chamber resembles neither the semicircle of the French National Assembly nor the long rectangle of the British House of Commons. The deputies to the *Bundestag* enter from a main corridor through any of three doors reserved for them and pass under the central public gallery. On two sides, in front of huge windows, two other galleries look down on the representatives—one for the diplomatic corps on the left, one for the press on the right. But it is of course in relation to the speaker's platform that the ideological classification of Left and Right is made—which means that the ambassadors can have a good look at the Christian Democrats, while the press sit close to the Social Democrats. As in the Palais Bourbon, the president of the assembly sits behind and above the speaker, at whose feet secretaries and stenographers busy themselves. Stretching out on either side of the president's seat is a long raised desk. On his right, facing the Social Democrats on the floor, the seats are reserved for interested members of the *Bundesrat*. On his left, with the Chancellor next to him, may sit members of the government. The difference in seating arrangement reflects an important institutional difference that has been politically, but not topographically, abolished with the Fifth Republic of General de Gaulle. It is not merely by chance that in Paris the members of the government sit in the first row of the deputies' benches, facing and slightly beneath the speaker, whereas in Bonn they seem to be placed like spectators on the sideline of the parliamentary game they actually dominate.

Legislative sessions are in general calm and rather tedious, especially since the disappearance in 1953 of the Communists and the extreme right. There are sometimes expressions of indignation from the floor, but these are more often feigned than real; there are stormy moments, too, but real passion is almost always missing. One of the reasons for this indifference is the lack of any uncertainty as to the outcome of a debate; party discipline is such that it is possible to predict a vote with almost complete accuracy. During the first two legislative sessions, for example, out of 288 roll-call votes, the "percentage of party loyalty" among the representatives in relation to the official stand taken by their parties was 99.8 per cent for the SPD, 94.5 per cent for the CDU, and 90.5 per cent for the FDP.

The function of the legislature to control the executive is fulfilled either when there is debate on a motion proposed in writing and signed by at least thirty delegates (*Grosse Anfrage*), or by the discussion of oral questions which are first submitted in writing no less than three days before the question period (*Fragestunde*). The opportunity for other representatives to ask additional questions permits, as in the House of Commons, a rapid and relatively complete discussion of a governmental proposal. As for the law-making function of the legislature, this is for the most part accomplished in committees rather than in plenary sessions. Certain committees meet as often as four times a week. They are made up of not less than fifteen members, who are assigned according to the relative size of their parties. Most committee meetings are neither public nor secret; nonmember representatives, ministers, members of the *Bundesrat*, and high officials have the right to attend; only the committees concerned with foreign affairs, the reunification issue, Berlin, defense, and the judiciary meet behind closed doors and in secret. Like hearings of American

Congressional committees, regular meetings are sometimes preceded by sessions open to the press and general public. Lobbyists for special interest groups (*Interessenvertreter*) and competent experts may be called to testify, in accordance with Article 73 of the Basic Law.

IV

Elections and Party Politics

PARLIAMENTARY life in the Federal Republic became considerably simplified in the years 1949–61, owing to a reduction of the number of parties. Increasingly, West German voters have concentrated their support on the Christian Democrats (CDU/CSU), the Social Democrats (SPD), and the Free Democrats (FDP). In the four legislative elections of 1949, 1953, 1957, and 1961, the three parties gained 72.1 per cent, 83.5 per cent, 89.7 per cent, and then 94.1 per cent of the total vote. (*See Table 4.*) One of the reasons for this growing simplification must be sought in West German election law, which encourages the citizen to vote "where it counts."

1. The Electoral System

West German elections are organized according to a system of proportional, personalized representation. The country is divided into 247 districts, and each district directly elects one representative by relative majority, as in Great Britain. But each elector must place two checks on his ballot. In one column he votes for a man, in the other for a party: The "direct" seats represent only half the total

Table 4. Four Legislative Elections

	August 14, 1949		September 6, 1953		September 15, 1957		September 17, 1961	
	Percentage of total vote	Number of seats won	Percentage of total vote	Number of seats won	Percentage of total vote	Number of seats won	Percentage of total vote	Number of seats won
Total number of registered voters	31,287,600		33,120,900		35,400,900		37,440,715	
Percentage of electorate voting	78.5		86.0		87.8		87.7	
CDU/CSU	31.0	139	45.2	243	50.2	270	45.4	242
SPD	29.2	131	28.8	151	31.8	169	36.2	190
FDP	11.9	52	9.5	48	7.7	41	12.8	67
DP	4.0	17	3.2	15	3.4	17	} 2.8	
Refugees	—		5.9	27	4.6			
Bavarian Party	4.2	17	1.7					
Extreme right	1.8	5	1.1		1.0		0.8	
Communist Party	5.7	15	2.2					
Neutralists	—		1.1				1.9	
Others	12.2	26	1.3	3	1.3			
Total	100.00	402	100.0	487	100.0	497	100.0	499

number of seats in Parliament; the other members of the *Bundestag* are chosen from lists drawn up in each *Land* by the political parties, the seats being distributed among the various parties' candidates in such a way that, in every *Land*, each party sends to the *Bundestag* a total number of deputies that corresponds to the percentage of votes it obtained in the "second column."*

What advantage, if any, accrues to the voter in his having two votes, one for the candidate, the other for the party of his choice? For the most part, he merely puts his X's in the same row and votes for the candidate presented by the party to which he gives his second vote. Yet it can happen that the district winner is not a representative of the party that gets the most votes, but only very rarely. More often,

* Take this theoretical example: In a *Land* where there are 20 seats to be filled and 10 districts, the Christian Democrat candidates come out ahead in 7 of the districts, the Social Democrats in 3, and the Free Democrats in none. On the second ballot, the parties obtain 50 per cent, 40 per cent, and 10 per cent of the votes respectively, a proportional division of 20 seats thus giving the parties 10, 8, and 2 representatives each. To their 7 directly elected seats, the CDU can therefore add 3 "list seats" (making 10); to their 3 seats, the SPD can add 5 "list seats" to make 8; and the FDP can add 2.

It can happen that a party will win more direct seats than it has a right to under the second-column mandate given for proportional division, since the directly elected seats represent half the total number only when counted, not in each *Land*, but in the whole country. (In Bavaria, there are 47 directly elected seats out of a total of 86, but in North Rhine-Westphalia there are only 66 out of 155.) For example, in Schleswig, in the election of 1961, when there were 14 districts and only 6 list seats to be filled, the CDU candidates won in 13 districts, but, in the *Land* as a whole, got only 42 per cent of the votes—as against 36 per cent for the SPD and 14 per cent for the FDP. Of the 20 available seats, then, the proportional division would give only 9 to the CDU, 8 to the SPD, and 3 to the FDP. What could be done to maintain the proportional strength of the parties? In this case, supplementary seats were awarded to the two smaller parties, while the CDU kept its 13 seats. Schleswig-Holstein therefore sent 24, instead of 20, deputies to the *Bundestag*, the 4 extra being called *Überhangsmandate*. A similar problem having arisen in the Saar over one seat, the *Bundestag* of 1961 numbered 499 deputies.

a comparison of the first and second votes will demonstrate the personal appeal of a given candidate to people in different political parties.

The system of proportional representation runs the serious risk of multiplying the number of parliamentary groups. However, to guard against this danger, the German electoral law stipulates that for a party to profit by proportional representation, it must have won a minimum of three direct seats or at least 5 per cent of the second votes on the national level. In 1961, only the CDU and the SPD fulfilled the first condition, winning 156 and 91 districts, respectively, and they of course also fulfilled the second. The FDP easily went beyond the 5 per cent minimum, but the All-German Party (GDP), with 2.8 per cent, and the German Peace Union (DFU), with 1.9 per cent are not represented in Parliament. Under a strict application of the proportional rule, they would have had 14 and 7 representatives, respectively, in the *Bundestag*. In the case of the refugee party (BHE), the effect of this proviso to the electoral law is even more clear. In the election of 1953, the BHE won 5.9 per cent of the party vote and earned 27 seats, but, four years later, it was down to 4.6 per cent and no seats. It is hardly surprising, therefore, that most of the BHE support went over in 1961 to the one party that had a chance of achieving the 5 per cent limit, the FDP.

2. Banning the Communist Party

The Basic Law is the first German constitution to confirm the existence of political parties. Article 21 reads:

1) The political parties participate in the forming of the political will of the people. They may be freely formed.

Their internal organization must conform to democratic principles. They must publicly account for the sources of their funds.

2) Parties which, by reason of their aims or the behavior of their adherents, seek to impair or destroy the free democratic basic order or to endanger the existence of the Federal Republic of Germany are unconstitutional. The Federal Constitutional Court decides on the question of unconstitutionality.

3) Details will be regulated by Federal legislation.

In fact, however, no law applying these strictures was ever drawn up, the principal difficulty being the matter of publicizing the sources of party funds. Only the SPD regularly publishes its accounts, although not in a very detailed manner with regard to the financing of its campaigns. The second section of Article 21, however, was used by the government in November, 1951, to ask the Court at Karlsruhe to pronounce on the cases of a small extreme right-wing party (SRP) and of the Communist Party (KPD). The judgments of unconstitutionality, bringing about the banning of both, were handed down on October 23, 1952, for the SRP and on August 17, 1956, for the KPD. If, in the latter case, judgment was so long in coming, it was because the defense used every possible means of delay and, above all, because the Court itself manifestly tried hard to hold back, if not actually to sidestep, a decision.

The Court's final opinions take up more than 300 pages in the collected documents of the Court's decisions. With elaborate care, the judges offered a detailed demonstration of the incompatability of Communism, founded on the dictatorship of the proletariat, and "the fundamental, liberal, and democratic order." But had not the four occupying powers authorized the existence of the KPD in 1945 as a democratic party? Quite true, the Court replied, but the notion of democracy on which they based their action was merely negative, since it was defined only by an anti-Nazi sentiment. The Basic Law, in contrast, had added a positive content to the concept of democracy, and it was in those terms that the KPD must be judged.

However, "a ban on the KPD is not juridically incompatible with the reauthorization of a Communist Party in the event of elections organized for the whole of Germany." By this, the Court meant to answer in advance, albeit rather unconvincingly, those who would see in the ban another obstacle to the goal of reunification.

The decision met with a lukewarm reception. It was frequently argued that the East German regime had been handed an excellent propaganda weapon on the issue of reunification and even on that of liberalism: The D.D.R. could now boast that in East Germany *they* tolerated the existence of a Christian Democratic Party and a Free Democratic Party—even if it was actually true that their members humbly followed the orders of the Communist rulers.

The liveliest criticisms were directed not at the Court but at the government. For, despite reservations expressed about certain aspects of the judgment, it was generally agreed that the Court could not but ban the Communist Party, if it did not wish to appear to absolve the Communist system of all taints of totalitarianism. The question remained, however, why the government had exerted such pressure on an obviously reluctant Court. And what kind of a victory was it—this banning of a political faction that was in any event slowly dying of its own accord? For, ever since 1946, the Communist Party had steadily been losing strength in relation to its power in prewar years. In the general elections of 1949, the KPD managed to pick up 5.7 per cent of the vote; by 1953, the figure had fallen to 2.2 per cent and the Party was eliminated from the *Bundestag*. Even in its best district, Remscheid-Solingen, it had only 12 per cent of the vote as against 21 per cent in 1949. The ban therefore seemed as ludicrous as a kick in the pants from a donkey. And it was at least as useful to the KPD as it was embarrassing. Now the Communists could proclaim, from East Germany, that if they were permitted to participate in the elections, then everyone could see what real support they had. On the other hand, it can hardly be said that the judgment at Karlsruhe has had any positive effect whatsoever on the cause of anti-Communism in the Federal Republic. If that cause was and is strong, it is for reasons that have nothing to do with the trial.

3. The Social-Democrat Opposition

The *Sozialdemokratische Partei Deutschlands*, founded in 1863, is by far the oldest political party in Germany. Already powerful, if not influential, in imperial Germany, it played a critical role in the years 1919–33. As long as the Weimar Republic lasted, the Socialist Party tried to "republicanize" the administration, the army, and the judiciary, as well as to obtain social reforms either by intense opposition efforts or by participating in coalitions with the bourgeois parties. Of the program it adopted at Heidelberg in 1925, that part which was theoretical and Marxist never held more than second place in the minds of German socialists. From 1928 to 1933, the party lost 2 million voters; but even in the elections of March 5, 1933, which were already controlled by the National-Socialist government, it got 18.3 per cent of the total vote. On the pretext that its leaders, who had escaped abroad, were trying to subvert the government, Hitler banned the SPD on June 23, 1933, and refused to seat its members in the *Reichstag*.

Emigration strongly affected the SPD, particularly because after 1945 there was reason to fear a public reaction against those socialist leaders who were not in Germany during the agony of its collapse and who had in many cases spent the war years in an enemy country. Therein lies one of the causes of a certain nationalistic hardening in the socialist stance since the war. In point of fact, fears of adverse political consequences stemming from the emigration proved ill founded. Several public-opinion polls have amply demonstrated the repugnance felt by the average German toward the *Emigrierte*, but this hostility was purely abstract and did not affect his feelings toward either Erich Ollenhauer, the late chairman of the SPD, or Willy Brandt, Mayor of Berlin since 1957, whose very name is a pseudonym he adopted while a refugee in Norway during the war. (A campaign of defamation against Brandt just before the election of 1961 had no appreciable effect on the outcome.)

On October 6, 1945, the socialist leaders who had survived the war met in the convent of Wenningsen, near Hanover, to prepare the reconstruction of their party. Three men dominated the discussions: Kurt Schumacher, who, since June, 1933, had been dragged from one concentration camp to another, but since his release in 1945 had set up a Socialist Party in the British zone; Erich Ollenhauer, who came from London as a representative of the Executive Committee of the party-in-exile; and Otto

Grotewohl, who came from Berlin, where he directed the Socialist Party in the Soviet zone. Grotewohl proposed the immediate formation of a new Executive Committee to prepare a merger with the Communist Party, but Schumacher, supported by Ollenhauer, had the election of a new committee put off until the party congress slated for the following year, and stipulated the complete independence of the Socialist Party. In reply, a United Socialist Party (SED) created by the merger of Socialists and Communists, was set up in the East on April 22, 1946. On May 10, the Congress of the SPD, meeting at Hanover, elected Schumacher and Ollenhauer as chairman and deputy chairman of a party that existed only in West Germany. For the Christian Democrats, the break between East and West would become effective only in December, 1947, and even then the eastern CDU did not cease to exist.

The SPD was not only the first political group to suffer from the division of Germany, but it was also the party that suffered the most from having to limit its recruitment to the western zones. For, until 1933, Prussia had been the stronghold of German socialism. Moreover, a sizeable number of the "Western" leaders of the SPD came from the East: Schumacher was a native of Kulm, south of Danzig; and Ollenhauer was born in Magdeburg. The SPD, then, was hurt to the quick by the division of Germany. None of this diminishes the fact that the SPD is the largest and best organized party in the Federal Republic; yet, even so, West Germany's economic prosperity has considerably reduced the people's interest in belonging to any organized group, including political parties: The number of SPD members, as well as the number of its local sections, has declined since 1947–48 (leveling off since 1955–56). At the end of

1947, the party numbered 875,000 members and had, a year later, 9,613 sections. These figures fell steadily to 580,-000 members and 7,000 sections and then climbed back slightly to 645,000 members and 7,770 sections at the end of 1961. In that year, the membership was roughly the same as it had been in 1951, but, in the meantime, the number of eligible voters had grown by about 5 million. Nevertheless, the SPD has twice the membership of the CDU and 50 per cent more than the French Communist Party. Somewhat less than 19 per cent of the members are women.

Three principal factors determine the ideological direction of the SPD: the need to get votes, the evolution of German industrial society, and the determination to oppose Communism. On the religious level, it finds its strongest support among Protestants. The SPD is not secular in the anticlerical French sense of the word, but it is sufficiently hostile toward any political influences of the church for most bishops and priests to recommend to their congregations that they should not vote for a party advocating a socialism condemned by the Popes. In reply, the SPD insists on the many similarities between its program and the encyclical *Mater et Magistra* of John XXIII.

But if *Mater et Magistra* marks a decisive turning point in the evolution of the church since the nineteenth century, by the same token the basic platform of the SPD (*Grundsatzprogramm*), which was adopted at a special congress at Bad Godesberg on November 15, 1959, is even further removed from Marxist doctrine or even from the SPD's 1925 program. Taking up a statement that had already been ratified by the 1954 Congress, the preamble to the new program asserted:

Democratic socialism—which in Europe has its roots in Christian ethics, in humanism, and in classical philosophy—does not claim to possess the eternal verities, and this not through lack of understanding or indifference to philosophical and religious truths, but through a respect for individual decision in matters of faith, a decision which must be determined neither by a political party nor by the state.

The program supports the idea of national defense, but calls for the banning of nuclear weapons in general and would specifically forbid their fabrication by the Federal Republic. If the section devoted to international affairs is somewhat short, the sections on social and economic matters are at once extensively developed and imprecise. The text calls for full employment—a perennial demand—but on a base of financial stability, because for a long time the SPD had been accused of being "the party of inflation." Beginning with the idea that the modern state of necessity profoundly influences the economy, the program goes on to propose a policy of joint forecasting and planning; but to this is added that "Free competition and the free initiative of the entrepreneur are important elements in Social-Democratic economic policy," and the final formula emerges as: "competition whenever possible—planning whenever necessary." The SPD wants to avoid *any* concentration of economic power, whether it be in the hands of private enterprise or the state. The program thus contains hints of nationalization, but also of decentralization.

But the key phrase, the phrase that reveals more than any other, figures in the last section of the program, called "Our Path": "From its beginnings as a party of the working class, the SPD has become a party of the whole people." Like the Labour Party in Britain and its equivalents in

Austria and Sweden, the SPD has had to try to attract a majority of voters in a country where workers have become more and more a minority class.

To succeed, a party program alone is not enough; leaders capable of appealing to a widely varied public are also necessary, as are the expensive procedures of a modern electoral campaign. The 1961 election cost the SPD an estimated 15.5 million DM, or about $3.9 million. Compared to the 1957 campaign, this one was more energetic and "scientific." The young and attractive mayor of Berlin, Willy Brandt, was the standard-bearer of the party in place of the rather pallid Erich Ollenhauer (who was, even so, an excellent party chairman). At the 1962 Congress, Brandt was elected deputy chairman. The election campaign of 1961 was conducted around him, and the whole world knew his name. When Erich Ollenhauer died on December 14, 1963, at the age of 62, mourned by all for his integrity, courage, and profound sense of democracy, the party could not avoid nominating Willy Brandt as his successor. At an extraordinary party congress held February 14–16, 1964, he was elected chairman, while the management of the party was turned over to one of the deputy chairmen, Herbert Wehner. The other deputy chairmanship was assumed by Fritz Erler, who is probably the most remarkable of all the socialist leaders for his enormous competence and his qualities as a statesman. The new leaders of the SPD have adopted, however, a tactic that, in the perspective of the 1965 elections, may bring bitter disillusionment: In order to acquire at least some of the clientele of the CDU, emphasis is being placed on what the two parties have in common, while criticism of the CDU is confined to details of the government's policy.

This strategy is not, perhaps, the best way to become the *Partei des Volkes* the SPD would like to be, by defeating the *Volkspartei* the CDU claims it is.

4. The CDU/CSU: The Dominant Party

The *Christlich-Demokratische Union* was brought into being on the initiative of a group of anti-Nazis who had been incarcerated in the Berlin prison of Moabit. This original group was made up of Catholic labor leaders, Protestants of various backgrounds, and members of the former Catholic *Zentrum* party. They wished to build a new Germany, a Germany whose society and economy would be profoundly transformed, completely purged of the poisons of National Socialism. Campaign necessities were to sully somewhat the purity of the first CDU program, but like the equally dizzying rise of the centrist Christian democratic parties in France, Belgium, and Italy, the rapid growth of the CDU was to a certain degree due to the lack of political formation that corresponded to the real desires of many of the voters. But such a situation cannot go on forever. For the party concerned, it ends of necessity when certain of its supporters are able to take their votes elsewhere: Either there is a serious reduction in the size of the vote, or there is a modification of its principles in accordance with the feelings of those voters it wishes to keep.

The social-economic program of the Christian Democrats in the British zone was adopted at Ahlen on February 9, 1947. Inspired by Karl Arnold, Minister-President of North Rhine-Westphalia, and by his trade-union and Catholic friends of the "left," it placed political freedom and economic liberation on the same plane. In calm language, it proclaimed the failure of capitalism and denounced monopoly. "State capitalism" was equally condemned. The program called for a planned economy under the direction of economic councils operating under the control of Parliament. At the opposite extreme, another Christian-Democrat program adopted in Düsseldorf on July 15, 1949, rejected all state planning, either in production, labor, or internal and external markets: It simply provided for governmental control of fiscal policy and for the regulation of imports. This was, in fact, an outline of the *Soziale Marktwirtschaft* that Erhard eventually put into effect. Its adoption was a clear victory for the "liberal" wing of the party over its "socialistic" wing.*

The "working group [*Arbeitsgemeinschaft*] CDU/CSU" is composed of two elements, of which one wished to be, and has remained, a separate organization. All official tallies of votes scrupulously distinguish between the two elements. In 1957, the CSU thus found itself in third place, defeating the Free Democrats on the basis of a 57.2 per cent share of the Bavarian vote. In 1961, the breakdown of votes put the SPD (11.4 million) ahead of the CDU (11.3 million), the Free Democrats (4 million), and the CSU, which, with slightly more than 3 million votes, still gained 50 seats in the *Bundestag* and 9.6 per cent of the votes of the *Bund*.

The President of the CSU since 1961 has been Franz-Josef Strauss, whose influence over the party was confirmed at the Congress of July, 1957, where he emerged unscathed from the attacks of a "clerical" who had been for many years the strongest personality in Bavaria, Dr. Alois Hund-

* See Chapter 3, Section 4.

hammer. But the party had been steadily, if slowly, becoming more "liberal" and more interdenominational since 1953. This goes far to explain its subsequent gains, but it is not certain that Strauss's energy and ambition reflect a spirit any more genuinely democratic than Hundhammer's disinterested authoritarianism. When Erhard became Chancellor late in 1963, Strauss started a kind of permanent opposition against his government, attacking mainly Schröder's foreign policies. In 1964, both this critical attitude to Erhard's cabinet (although four members of it are CSU members) and other internal tensions have made the CSU position a unique and special one in German politics.

Cut off from Bavaria, the CDU is, in any case, a thoroughly decentralized party, and is singular in having achieved success in a national election although it did not exist as a unified organization; the CDU held its first federal congress only in October, 1950, at Goslar. The party is composed of sixteen federations, including one in West Berlin—which are the result of the party's having been organized originally in *Land* parties (*Landesparteien*) years before the birth of the federal party. North Rhine-Westphalia has two federations, Lower Saxony three, and Baden-Württemberg four. To these one must add two others, more symbolic than real, one for the Soviet zone (Exil-CDU) and one for the eastern territories (Oder-Neisse CDU). The refugee members of these organizations are for the most part enrolled in the local section at their place of residence in the Federal Republic. The CDU has more than 4,000 of these local sections, but their character varies tremendously from region to region. Sometimes they are well organized and have a large membership (certainly about 5,000 in Essen and Cologne), and sometimes they are

merely an office. This is because in one place the CDU may
have strong mass support, while in another it may be only
a party of a small, influential élite (though often it is both
at the same time). In all, the membership figure reaches
about 300,000.

The CDU is a truly nondenominational party, in contrast
to the prewar *Zentrum*, which had very little Protestant
representation. But this nondenominational character of the
party as a whole appears in a different light depending on
where one looks. CDU Protestants are proportionally
higher where the population numbers fewer Catholics. In
Schleswig, for example, which is 88 per cent Protestant,
the CDU appears as a Christian party and can pick up a good
50 per cent of the votes, while elsewhere the party appears
as a more strictly Catholic one. Yet it is true that Catholics
are overrepresented in its organization, and that its militants
tend to be Catholic in most regions. This phenomenon is
best explained by the comparatively easy integration of
Catholics into confessional movements that dispose them
toward militancy. But among the leading politicians and
government ministers, the situation is quite different. The
CDU wishes its image to be strictly nondenominational.
Since 1951, there has been a Protestant committee
(*Evangelischer Arbeitskreis*) within the CDU/CSU whose
chairman, since 1955, has been Gerhard Schröder, once
Minister of the Interior in the Adenauer government and
now Foreign Minister in Erhard's cabinet. Born in 1910,
Schröder is one of those who may legitimately aspire to
succeed Erhard if the latter is not successful as Chancellor.
(As a potential successor to Adenauer, Schröder had been
too young, with not enough prestige. The lack of prestige
also held for the older Protestant leaders of the CDU, espe-

cially the president of the *Bundestag*, Eugen Gertsenmaier.)

Now it was clear that the second chancellor should be a Protestant—Adenauer was a Catholic and so was President Lübke—but the Protestant Erhard can hardly succeed Adenauer as chairman of the party: Only a Catholic can really become head of the CDU. For this post, the two candidates most often mentioned were Heinrich von Brentano, the party's parliamentary leader from 1949 to 1955, and again as of 1961, and Heinrich Krone, who was parliamentary leader from 1955 to 1961, and since then a minister of state. It was Krone, the respected but not brilliant former leader of the *Zentrum*, whom Adenauer would have liked to have seen as President of the Republic in 1959, and whom he preferred over Erhard as the future head of government. But in the party congress of May, 1962, a new star appeared in the skies of the CDU/CSU. Josef-Hermann Dufhues, the Catholic Minister of the Interior in North Rhine-Westphalia, was made national party chairman. Although he was born in 1908, Dufhues was considered the leader of the Young Turks who wanted to reorganize and strengthen the party. But he seems farther away from leadership today than he was two years ago, for his reorganization of the party structure failed. He has at least one young rival in Rainer Barzel, 40 years old, Minister for All-German Affairs from December, 1962, until October, 1963, when he became acting chairman of the CDU *Bundestag* faction when von Brentano became ill. The internal divisions of the CDU, however—on Berlin, on the relationship with de Gaulle, on strategy against the SPD—have finally induced the party congress to re-elect Adenauer.

The problems of leadership are important—but problems

of money no less so. The financial affairs of the CDU have none of the clarity of those of the SPD. It is certain that the public contributions are not even sufficient to pay for normal party functioning. Constant propaganda and election campaigns depend on private donations—which are sometimes direct and sometimes indirect. Of the latter, a good example might be the case of a corporation placing a large number of subscriptions with an expensive party magazine. There is even a Contributors' Association (*Stifterverband*) which helps out all nonsocialist parties—with the CDU getting the lion's share. Nevertheless, it has not succeeded in eliminating the Free Democrats.

5. Bipartisanship?

The Free Democrats are in fact the only serious competition for the two larger parties. The others have not completely disappeared, but they have steadily lost strength over the years. The Bavarian Party (*Bayern Partei*), which was important in 1949, has been almost entirely gobbled up by the CSU. The extreme right, under various titles, never really succeeded in getting even a hand-hold on the electorate. And despite the SPD's "*embourgeoisement*" and "Atlanticism," no group has been able to find any room to its left. The *Gesamtdeutsche Volkspartei* (GVP) of Dr. Heinemann, a former CDU minister, and Frau Wessel, a former president of the *Zentrum*, was dissolved in 1957, and its leaders have become Social-Democrat representatives. The *Deutsche Friedensunion* (German Peace Union) followed the GVP without achieving any particular successes. The successful integration of the refugees into the West German economy caused the decline of the *Bund*

der Heimatvertriebenen und Entrechteten (Union of Expellees and Victims of Injustice) which had vainly transformed itself into a *Gesamtdeutscher Bloc* (All-German
Bloc). In 1961, the GB/BHE joined forces with a small
right-wing party—the *Deutsche Partei*—which had managed to be represented in the legislatures of 1949, 1953, and
1957, only because it had the support of the CDU. But
while they had totalled 3.7 million votes as separate parties,
their union in the new *Gesamtdeutsche Partei* (GDP) in
1961 could only pull together a mere 570,000 votes. A
breakdown of the vote by district shows that the majority
of former GB/BHE voters went over to the Free Democrats, thus exercising on that party a strong pull to the
right.

The *Freie Demokratische Partei* was formed as a unified
party in the three western zones of occupation as late as 1948,
and it did not hold a national congress until June, 1949.
In the Soviet zone, a liberal democratic party (LDP) had
been set up in 1945. In Württemberg-Baden, a popular
democratic party (LDP) was created in January, 1946. In
later years, it became a regional organization of the FDP,
though keeping its original name.

At first, the FDP was the party of liberal republicans,
inspired by the traditions of the Revolution of 1848, and of
the bourgeois right-wing, who wished to see economic
liberalism entirely restored in Germany. The unfortunate
ambiguity of the word "liberal," however, permitted the
party leaders to leave more or less in the shadows the distinction between political liberties and free enterprise. The
first component of FDP thought, the tradition of 1848, was
well rooted in southwest Germany and with such men as
Reinhold Maier and President Heuss himself. The second

had its center of gravity in the Ruhr; Vice-Chancellor Franz Blücher was one of its foremost representatives, and he presided over the party after Heuss was elected chief of state in 1949.

Beginning in 1952, the FDP was wracked by several internal crises arising from questions of personality, policy, and politics. More or less hamstrung in 1957–61, when the CDU had an absolute majority, the Free Democrats have played a larger role since the elections of 1961 placed them in a position where they hold the balance of parliamentary power. Since January, 1960, the party has been led by Erich Mende, a Silesian Catholic. Despite the "modernizing" influence of Mende's "Düsseldorf wing" of the party, the FDP is very much to the right of the Christian Democrats in social and economic affairs.

In maintaining this position lies the party's best chance for the future. For, in order to hold its own against the rise of the Social Democrats, the CDU is now forced to present to the public as "social" an image as possible, which may disenchant its conservative wing. At the same time, the FDP remains attractive for those politically liberal voters who do not want to support one of the two dominant parties.

But, will West Germany eventually find itself with a real two-party system? Under an electoral system like the British one, this would have come about long since. Under the German system, it is not impossible, but improbable. Table 5 reveals that the youngest voters, even if they almost completely spurn the smaller parties, feel a certain attraction for the FDP. The table is at once encouraging and discouraging for the Social Democrats. The generation to whom the SDP will always be "Red," whatever it does, is giving way to another in which there are more socialist voters than Christian-Democrat. But this is true only of the men; women voters of all ages swing the balance in favor of the CDU. Certainly, the influence of the churches is important here, but it does not explain everything, especially since there have recently been certain changes in the Catholic vote, and the Protestant vote has always been fairly well spread out.

TABLE 5. PARTY VOTES IN THE 1961 ELECTIONS, BROKEN DOWN ACCORDING TO SEX AND AGE

	CDU/CSU	SPD	FDP	Others
Percentage of all men voters	40.3	39.7	13.6	6.4
Percentage of all women voters	49.6	32.9	12.2	5.3
Percentage of men voters under 30	43.0	41.0	12.2	3.8
Percentage of women voters under 30	49.5	34.8	11.9	3.8
Percentage of men voters, 30–59	38.2	40.7	14.4	6.7
Percentage of women voters, 30–59	47.9	33.7	12.8	5.6
Percentage of men voters, 60 and over	43.4	35.9	12.9	7.8
Percentage of women voters, 60 and over	53.7	29.7	10.9	5.7

Source: *Wirtschaft und Statistik*, February, 1962.

Indeed, a number of public-opinion polls conducted at regular intervals has shown the beginnings of a sort of "window-shopper's attitude" among loyal supporters of both parties. Whereas 76 per cent of the Catholic vote would have gone to the CDU in 1953, the percentage dropped to 72 in 1957 and to 61 in 1961. Whereas 71 per cent of union members would have voted for the SPD in

1953, the percentages were 68 in 1957 and 65 in 1961. This leveling tendency is perfectly normal when, as in the United States, two major parties want to appeal to the whole population and find themselves separated only by the most subtle nuances, rather than by a fundamental cleavage. It could be, of course, that an economic crisis will provoke new conflicts; but, for the moment, almost all Germans are casting their votes for parties that are sensible, politically liberal, and, whatever their original doctrine, ideologically affected by a continuing prosperity.

V

The Ideology of Prosperity

THE monetary reform of June 20, 1948, marked the spectacular debut of an economic renaissance in West Germany. Production began to gather speed. In 1946, the index had been at 33 in relation to a 1936 level at 100. In the summer of 1949, when the Federal Republic came into being, production was already up to 90 on the index. Yet, this was not prosperity: Unemployment figures were also growing, and there was a serious deficit in the balance of payments. During the next ten years, however, production went up by 126 per cent, and, despite a rapid growth in the work force, unemployment disappeared. In September, 1950, there were 1.58 million unemployed as against 13.83 million salaried workers; by September, 1961, there were 95,000 unemployed as against 20.93 million at work. From then on, German employers found it necessary to import foreign labor, and by mid-1964, nearly 1 million non-Germans were employed in the Federal Republic.

West Germany's balance of trade became favorable in 1952, and, by 1961, the value of exports over imports—which themselves had quadrupled—attained 6.6 billion

DM. By March 6, 1961, the surplus in the balance of payments had reached such proportions that a revaluation of the mark became necessary (although the surplus reached the 6 billion DM again in 1963); the country was also able to pay off the debts incurred immediately after the war. The population's standard of living rose steadily. The motorcycle replaced the bicycle, and the auto now is replacing the motorcycle. The consumption of potatoes has declined while that of coffee has risen from a little less than a pound per person in 1950 to 6.4 pounds in 1960; and the cigarette, which was used virtually in the place of money during the famine years, became less and less a luxury: Each German over fifteen smoked 630 cigarettes in 1950, 1,643 in 1960.

Are these the indications of an "economic miracle"? What were the factors that contributed to a development of such extraordinary proportions? To what extent can one credit that one particular economic policy called "a social market economy"? Is this policy really "social" or really "liberal"? If it is true that an economic philosophy dictated the development of the government's economic policy, has not the very success of that policy dictated a kind of dominant ideology in the Federal Republic? These are a few of the important questions to which we can only give some elements of an answer.

1. Germany's Trump Cards

German industry after the defeat was immobilized, but it was not destroyed. Its production was so feeble, the physical destruction so obvious, that one might have thought that Germany had been fatally wounded at its very heart. It was not. Though its towns and cities were indeed in ruins, the steel industry was only 10 per cent destroyed, the chemical industry from 10 to 15 per cent incapacitated, the machine industry from 15 to 20 per cent, and the textiles industry 20 per cent. Recovery became possible, therefore, as soon as the monetary chaos was overcome. In a sense, Germany has been in a similar situation three times within twenty-five years. In 1923, 1930, and 1945, the country appeared to be overcome by economic catastrophe, but industrial capacity had in none of the three cases been totally impaired. Once the financial mess had been straightened out, there was a startling expansion in production (industry having been, in fact, a beneficiary of the monetary collapse). The recovery of 1948, like that of 1924, was effected for the benefit of state and industry and, since the currency reform reduced indebtedness to insignificance, at the expense of the provident.

The Allies had declared that they intended to levy reparations and to shackle the development of German industry. Certainly the reparations restricted German industry, and the dismantling of factories did continue until 1950. Yet one can hardly say that the Federal Republic has been crushed under the weight of reparation. Until about 1952, West Germany emphasized its poverty in order to evade the problem. Afterward, it was really too late in the game to talk about such a timeworn issue. This process of double-reasoning was particularly obvious in the Saar affair. The German-Israeli Treaty of 1952 is an exception, however.* As for shackling German production, this idea completely disappeared with the inauguration of the Schu-

* See below, Chapter VII.

man Plan. On the economic ledger, in fact, the intervention of the victorious powers must be put on the credit side, for the German recovery was greatly helped by American aid. The billions of dollars in loans and especially in gifts (coming at first in the form of GARIOA funds—special aid to occupied territories—then as the Marshall Plan) played a decisive role, all the more so in that West Germany, unlike Great Britain and France, was neither engaged in a colonial war nor obliged to keep a standing army, nor were there any former German colonies to aid.

To be sure, there were, until 1955, the occupation expenses to be paid. But, even if one concedes that the 7.2 billion DM that West Germany had to pay each year were wholly devoted to and used up in unproductive expenses, which is not the case; even if one leaves out the considerable influx of dollars paid into the economy by American troops, the proportion of national revenue West Germany has devoted to defense has been consistently lower than that of her three major enemies in the last war. Military expenses for 1960–61 represented 3.8 per cent of West Germany's gross national product, a burden even lower than that of Belgium, Denmark, or Italy, and two or three times lower than that of Great Britain or the U.S.A. But here, the German government found itself in a difficult situation: If West Germany were to rearm quickly, she would seriously alarm other countries. If, however, she stretched out the duration of the Allied restrictions on the *Bundeswehr*—as she in fact did do—then she would appear to be leaving it to others to make the sacrifices she herself claimed were necessary for Western defense. In any case, military expenditures have increased by 48 per cent between 1961 and 1963.

At first, overpopulation in the Federal Republic was a

terrible handicap. In 1939, 39.4 million persons lived in the area of the present West Germany, or 160 persons per square kilometer. In 1946, there were 43.7 million, in 1950 47.7 million, in 1956 50.6 million—to which were added in 1957 the million persons living in the Saar. By 1960, the population was 53.4 million, or 215 persons per square kilometer. But these total figures of population growth from 1939 to 1950 are deceiving. It is necessary to remember that the number of people able to work grew by only 10 per cent whereas the population as a whole increased by 33 per cent. The war left behind 1.5 million invalids, of which half were 50 per cent or more incapacitated, as well as almost a million widows. Still, these problems were to a great extent compensated for by the economic advantages accruing to the arrivals of millions of refugees from the East who were determined to work hard to remake their lives. They constituted a labor force that was at once cheap and plentiful, that helped to speed up West German recovery, once it had begun, as much as it helped to slow down the rise in wages. The refugees, after seeming to pose an insurmountable obstacle to German recovery, have been at the same time a great burden and magnificent stimulus to the German economy.

The German people have worked hard, not because they are Germans, but because they wished to lift themselves out of misery and chaos. In 1959, of thirteen industrial sectors studied by the statistical services of the European Common Market, the average work week was lower in Germany than in Italy in twelve sectors, and in nine sectors as compared with France. The major sacrifice German labor had made was to have accepted the basic decision that Erhard made in 1949: to grant absolute priority to considerations of economic development, not in order to satisfy the demands of the consumer, but to benefit production and West Germany's foreign trade. According to the Minister of Economic Affairs, consumer benefits would follow automatically.

This basic principle differed from that adopted in France in 1945, but corresponded to the Soviet choice favoring an economy of producers rather than an economy of consumers. On the other hand, the liberal component in the German policy favored the strong, the dynamic, the "entrepreneurs," a term that was to regain its full etymological significance at the same time as the socio-economic class it designates rose to the apex of German society. The unemployed, the wounded veterans, received only the smallest aid while the *nouveaux riches* began to wallow in almost insolent luxury. But did this wealth deprive others of goods and well-being that could have been theirs under a different policy? Erhard did not think so. For him, the profit motive was the best possible stimulus to economic recovery—but on one condition: The tax-deductible restaurant bills, the enjoyment of luxurious automobiles at company expense— this sort of thing should absorb only a small part of the entrepreneur's revenue. For the system to function properly, it was necessary that most of the profits be plowed back into the business in the form of productive investments. In other words, the drive for even greater profits and the desire for economic prosperity must remain stronger than the desire for enjoyment. The bet as to whether they would was, in the main, won. As Erhard hoped, industrial development was accomplished with a minimum of indebtedness, thanks to a particularly important system of self-financing.

2. Soziale Marktwirtschaft

There remains the question of whether the work force has been the beneficiary of this governmental policy, or whether, as the opposition says, it has been the victim. If one takes 1950 as the year of reference at 100 on the index, then the cost of living in 1961 was at 121 and gross hourly wages were at 225, which corresponds to a rise in real wages of 83 per cent. But the gross hourly wages represented were in 1960 only 60.8 per cent of the national revenue as against 59.1 per cent in 1950, while at the same time the number of people in the labor force rose by 39 per cent. In other words, the individual wage-earner's slice of the national economic pie diminished. The loss was, however, made up for little by little by the rapid rise in real wages since 1960, which has made the German worker one of the best paid in Europe. The financial authorities are still rather disturbed by this development, though. In effect, the West German government today faces a problem on which French governments have foundered during the whole postwar period: how to avoid inflation and at the same time expand production under full employment.

Welfare costs in Germany are about the same as in the other countries of the Common Market. In 1959, the money set aside for social security amounted to 17.6 per cent of the national revenue, while it was 16.4 per cent in France. And if direct aid to growing families was almost nonexistent (0.4 per cent, as against 4.5 per cent in France), old-age and veterans' payments were far higher (8.3 per cent, as against 4 per cent). At the same time, the intervention of the state makes itself felt more directly than under the French system. In 1959, social security costs were financed as follows:

	Insured Individuals	Employers	The Government	Other
Federal Republic	36.7%	40.5%	18.6%	4.2%
France	19.4	68.8	5.3	6.5

Legislative or governmental action has been felt equally in two areas in which the results have exceeded even the most optimistic predictions: public housing and the integration of refugees.

It is true that the financing of new housing became proportionally less and less the business of the state. In 1950, 1.7 billion DM for housing came from public funds and 1.6 billion from private capital, but, by 1961, these figures had changed respectively to 3.2 and 10.3 billion. But a law of April 24, 1950—supplemented by another on March 14, 1957—was responsible for the construction of 3.5 million units of "social housing." Since 1953, the rate of 500,000 housing units per year has been exceeded. The Federal Republic doubtless leads the whole world in the number of dwellings built per one thousand persons. The rate was 10.3 in 1960, as opposed to 9.5 in Switzerland, 9.1 in Sweden, 7.4 in Norway and Holland, and 7 in France. Whereas, in 1950, only one building in twenty was a postwar construction, the ratio was one out of three by the end of 1958. Those Germans who are still poorly housed may justifiably say to themselves that they need not wait too long for normal lodgings. Here indeed is cause for satisfaction, and a reason for the West Germans' positive attitude toward their country's future development, in contrast with the situation in France. Moreover, from the beginning, this liberal state has had recourse to measures designed to prevent insufficient utilization of the new housing.

Thus, there grew up in the Federal Republic a sense of solidarity that, if it was stronger during times of trouble than in time of prosperity, was still strong enough to permit the smooth functioning of a so-called "equalization of the burden" (*Lastenausgleich*) instituted by a law of August 14, 1952. At the end of 1961, more than 42 billion DM had been transferred, according to an extremely complex system of rules, to various very different categories of the social dependents listed in the law: refugees of 1945, emigrants of 1933, original inhabitants of West Germany who suffered war damages, those who had saved their personal holdings and been nearly ruined by the monetary reform. Loans for housing, furniture, and pensions were equally varied, the most important, however, being the principal indemnification for reclassification. Financing of this equalization was taken care of by a seemingly Draconian rule: Except for certain public organizations—the central banks and religious and charitable institutions—every capable person was required to give half of all he possessed for the redistribution and equalization. The point of departure, however, was the tax base in the lean year 1948–49; people and companies have only to pay their share in quarterly payments spread over thirty years.

This "sharing of the burden" was only one of many methods used to speed the economic integration of the refugees. A whole series of steps was taken to assure what has surely been the most remarkable success of the Federal Republic, even if the official statistics contain a deceptive element: Among the 13.5 million expellees and refugees numbered as of January 1, 1961, were counted not only that group of Germans who before 1939 lived east of the Oder-Neisse, in the Sudeten, or in present East Germany, but also their children born since 1939, and notably those who have come into the world in West Germany since 1945.

Economic integration is not, however, equivalent to psychological assimilation. Tensions between native-born and refugee have been very strong, especially in the country, but even in the factories of Württemberg there exists a kind of real if intangible segregation. The "proletarianization" of many former peasants, artisans, shop-keepers, and small industrialists has obviously been a difficult factor in the process of adaptation. The younger generation evidently encounters less difficulty and has recourse to that best means of assimilation—marriage. The proportion of marriages between native-born and refugee is growing steadily. But the favorable course of the process of assimilation is hindered by another factor the importance of which should not be underestimated: contradictions in government policy. Would not a real assimilation of refugees be tantamount to a tacit recognition of the Oder-Neisse line? For this reason, the government encourages the various groups and associations that demand a return to their native land— whether it was German territory in 1937 or not.

One might well ask then if the numerous votes the refugees cast for the CDU have been motivated solely by economic satisfaction, if they have really been an expression of thanks for a successful integration. What has been the political effect of that hope to return to territories which lie, some of them, far beyond the 1937 frontiers? Whatever the answer, it is wise not to overestimate the refugee groups. If economic prosperity continues, if no depression occurs to bring back serious unemployment, the integration process will go on, and along with it, an assimilation that will be all the more permanent as the younger generation reaches maturity. Each year of economic expansion dampens the explosive political power of the refugee problem and more and more transforms these people into normal members of West German society.

Real wages have increased. The housing problem is on the way to being solved. The refugees have been integrated. Yet it is impossible to speak of a real social policy in West Germany. The "extensive social program" that was promised in a governmental declaration of October, 1953, has never seen the light of day. At best, the most pressing needs are met; at worst, vote-getting gifts in the form of definite but limited measures are issued three months before elections. The structures of society are never in jeopardy. As in France, the number of working-class children who attain a higher education does not exceed 5 per cent; as in France, there is a shortage of educational facilities and good teachers. Under the "social market economy," the accent is on the economic rather than the social.

But is this really a market economy? In theory, state intervention in the economy is exercised only in the interests of free competition and for the protection of the consumer. But the government does in fact participate more and more directly in economic life, both by means of subsidies (5.4 billion DM in 1962, including 1.9 billion for agriculture, and this does not count social security) and through publicly owned enterprises, which, in 1958, furnished 36.7 per cent of the iron ore, 25.7 per cent of the coal, 70.1 per cent of the crude aluminum, 45.2 per cent of the zinc, and 40.3 per cent of the automobiles. (Since then, the Volkswagen works have been turned over to the private sector through a stock issue.) But private commercial and industrial combines have not been eliminated by the law "against restrictions of free competition" that was passed on July 4, 1957, after seven years of furious struggle. The antitrust bureau instituted by that law has scarcely any effectiveness whatsoever.

3. The Economy Above All?

While it is true that Erhard was not able to get open public support for his war against the combines, is it not also true that antitrust legislation—like the measures taken to break up the chemical and steel industries—was an idea of the occupying powers? Most Germans, in fact, were convinced that the Allies' principal goal was not to democratize their economy but to weaken it. Moreover, they had vetoed the nationalization of the coal industry proposed by the *Landtag* of North Rhine-Westphalia in 1947. Erhard, in the name of economic efficiency, was opposed to deconcentration, but he was favorably disposed to the fight against the combines in the name of a free price system. For the general public, however, the distinction between the two was not easy to grasp. In 1938, six *Konzerne* alone produced 95 per cent of the steel, 98 per cent of the pig-iron, and controlled 42 per cent of coal production in the Ruhr. The Allied measures taken against the combines ended by splitting them into forty-five steel, coal, and commercial companies. But, from 1952 on, signs of re-concentration began to appear, as much in the name of economic principles as by the return to power of the old families. The creation of the European

Coal and Steel Authority also helped the process along, for how could the High Authority in Luxembourg refuse the German steel industry the right to be as centralized as the French? In December, 1954, the ECSA authorized the reconstitution of the Mannesmann group. The Konzern Stinnes, dominated by the Hugo Stinnes corporation of Baltimore, controls an impressive number of enterprises of all kinds. Alfried Krupp arranged matters differently, however. He ignored coal and steel and, thanks to the indemnities paid his company, became extraordinarily strong in the machine industry and in naval construction. (He has specialized in equipment for underdeveloped countries.) Theoretically, the power of the directors of these companies and cartels is limited: A law of May 21, 1951, required that in every coal and steel enterprise employing more than 1,000 workers, there be a system of comanagement between employers and employees; this system was later extended to the holding companies.

The law turned over the management of each company to two groups, a Surveillance Council (*Aufsichtsrat*), which fills the function of a legislature and has eleven members, and a Board of Directors (*Vorstand*), of three members, which is in a sense the executive. The eleven members of the *Aufsichtsrat* are chosen as follows: Four represent the owner or owners, and four the workers. A fifth member, who may not belong to the company nor have any financial interest in it, is added to each group of four. The eleventh man is named by agreement between the workers' and owners' groups. As for the *Vorstand*, its three members, who are of equal status, are the commercial director, the technical director, and the *Arbeitsdirektor* (literally, "work-director," but in fact social director). The latter may be neither nominated nor licensed by the Surveillance Council without the consent of a majority of the five workers' representatives. In addition, a law on company organization of October 11, 1952, allows the workers' representatives a certain share in not only the social but also the economic management of all enterprises. Is this not going rather far toward a weakening of the economically powerful?

To put the question another way, who has the economic power in this prosperous society? "There is no problem," the government would reply. "But there is one," answer the unionists. At the tenth anniversary of the *Bundesverband der Deutschen Industrie* (the equivalent of the NAM) in October, 1959, Adenauer declared:

Under the leadership of President Berg, the BDI has been a faithful auxiliary in the accomplishment of these great and difficult tasks. I would like to say here a word of very warm thanks to the whole of the BDI. I would like publicly to bear witness that this group has always clearly understood the interdependence between that part of the economy that it represents and the other parts of the German economy— including the interdependence between the economy and our social problems. I feel also that I should call attention to the fact that President Berg has never in the course of the last ten years ceased to set a high example for these great relations. . . . He has never been the representative of special interests, and above all not of the special interests of heavy industry.

But Ludwig Rosenberg, vice-president and later president of the German Federation of Trade Unions, shortly afterward stated:

From 1 to 2 per cent only of West German businesses dispose of more than a million DM in capital. This 1 or 2 per cent control half the country's production and distribution. For the very existence of a democratic state, it is intolerable that such a concentration of economic power be authorized under this form and even encouraged by fiscal legislation and other measures. The presence of an analogous development in other countries is of little consolation to us.

In reality, the question may certainly be asked in a different way. Which sector should have the ascendancy—the economic or the political? In a rather curious fashion, the Federal Republic gives a two-fold answer, which is at once unanimous and contradictory. In the first place, the prosperity achieved during the time of "the social market economy" has transformed into a kind of dogma the virtues of economic liberalism, now widely identified with those of freedom itself. It is significant that in the decision of the Federal Constitutional Court that outlawed the Communist Party, one finds an image of democratic society that corresponds to the image classical liberalism held of society, namely, that it is divided into groups that are involved in the free play of forces but that it excludes the domination of any one group over the others. The idea that the "democratic and liberal" order could itself correspond to a situation of domination is not even examined. In this perspective, the role of the state is not to channel and influence but to permit free competition both in politics and economics, the latter being the decisive factor in the progress of the whole society. From this, there follows a basic opposition to all ideas of planning* and nationalization, and, above all,

*See below, Chapter 7.

the conviction that economics is the really creative force in society, leaving to politics the role of umpire. This ideology was all the more convincing to West Germans in that the autonomy of the economic sector, the unobtrusiveness of the state, and the renunciation of all attempts to transform the structures of the society very soon appeared to the great majority of the people to be fundamental elements of that freedom that distinguished the Federal Republic from the other Germany.

In effect—and this is the second part of the answer—politics comes into its own when it is a question of defense against the East. A simple example will point up the contradiction. In its quadrennial report of 1961, the Advisory Committee to the Ministry of All-German Affairs, which has members from the unions and the Social Democratic Party, declared in a unanimously adopted report that they

> were guided by the principle that a unified Germany must have a liberal economic and social order. . . . One of the most important tasks of the economic reunification is to change the various enterprises in the Soviet zone of occupation so as to render them effective in a market economy (*markwirtschaftlich aktionsfähig*); to achieve this, the restoration of a self-responsible (*selbstverantwortlich*) group of owners is of great importance.

Yet, on the preceding page, the Committee stated that East Germany does 85 per cent of its trade with the Eastern bloc, while 95 per cent of the foreign trade of West Germany is carried on with countries which are not part of that bloc.

The ideal order, then, is founded on the free play of

private forces. Yet this free play is completely transformed by the pressure of political facts decided at the state level. There is no need here to elaborate on a difficulty that is not peculiar to Germany, but it is true that if there, the problem goes particularly deep.

VI

The Social and Moral Order

THE citizen is not simply a voter—or, more precisely, not simply an independent individual who stands alone and helpless, observing the behavior of political parties in order to decide how he will vote the next time. Nor is he simply an isolated farmer, for instance, or worker. He also belongs to one or several groups that influence him and to which in turn he can contribute his own ideas. Even if he should remain apart from these groups, they will claim nonetheless to speak in his name. A railroad worker, for example, who is also a newspaper reader and a Catholic, finds himself "represented" not only by the men whom he elects to the *Bundestag*—the "representatives of the people" —but by his union, by the Church, and by the organ of public opinion that the press desires to be. We cannot here draw up a complete inventory of the groups and forces in the Federal Republic that at the same time speak for and influence the citizen, and that influence the conduct of public affairs. But we can examine some of the most important.

1. The Unions

At the end of the war, the Allies had actively encouraged the rebirth of the trade-union movement, which they felt could be their strongest ally in the job of democratizing Germany. The union leaders who began organizing after the war were many of them the same men who had been in the vanguard of the labor movement before 1933. Two factors led them to work together for a unified labor front: the shared experience of tragedy, for the Nazi persecution had affected the entire labor movement regardless of its internal differences; and the necessity of presenting a common front vis-à-vis the victorious powers. Once the occupation zones had been done away with, a constitutive assembly was held in Munich, October 12–14, 1949. From it was born the *Deutscher Gewerkschaftsbund*, or German Federation of Trade Unions (DGB), with headquarters in Düsseldorf. The most respected of the surviving prewar leaders of the movement, Hans Böckler, was elected to the presidency.

At first glance, the structure of the DGB closely resembles that of the big central labor organization in France; the sixteen *Gewerkschaften* would correspond to the French *fédérations d'industrie*, and the eight *Landesbezirke* would correspond to the French *unions départementales*. In reality, however, there are major differences. Even the terminology is different. In France, the fundamental unit is the local professional or craft group. It is this which, properly speaking, constitutes a union, "*le syndicat*." In West Germany, the corresponding unit is only a section or subsection of the basic organization that groups together all the workers in a particular branch of industry. To translate the initials

I.G.* (*Industrie-Gewerkschaft*) by "industrial federation" is therefore misleading, even with reference to a particular commodity, for unlike many federations, the *Industrie-Gewerkschaften* are centralized, hierarchical organizations and this constitutes one of the elements of their power.

Despite the care that was taken not to give too much influence to the large *Gewerkschaften*, they still occupy a very privileged position. The quasi-equal representation they enjoy on the executive committee of the DGB does not apply in the congress, where, generally speaking, each federation may send one delegate per 15,000 members— a representation that assures a constant majority for three of the unions out of the total sixteen: I. G.-Metall (metal-workers), I. G.-Bergbau (miners) and ÖTV (public services and transport workers). These three unions also possess exceptionally large financial resources. It is the federations that collect members' dues (of which 15 per cent went to the central organization from 1949 to 1952, and 12 per cent since then, to which must be added the quarterly contributions made to a central Solidarity Fund). A union member's dues are set at the value of one hour's work per week. Since wages are especially high in the metal industry, the I.G.-Metall, with 1.6 million members, contributes about one-third of the DGB budget, which has reached about $10 million.

At its inception, the DGB had 4.9 million members. In 1952, it had passed the 6 million mark, but since then the membership has grown hardly at all. At the end of 1961, it included 5.13 million laborers, 724,000 salaried workers, and 528,000 government employees, for a total of 6.4 mil-

---

* Not to be confused with the I. G. in I. G.-Farben, for instance, which means "*Interessen Gemeinschaft.*"

lion members. Given the rapid growth of the labor force in West Germany, the proportion of union members has steadily dropped. There are many reasons for this apparent disaffection with the labor movement. Affluence is not a good stimulant to union militancy; the advantages of prosperity often seem to have come about quite naturally and are in any case shared by members and nonmembers alike (a fact that caused the Miners Federation to propose a mandatory "solidarity" contribution from all workers to the union, as in Sweden and Switzerland). Furthermore, for a good many of the workers, the DGB has become an immense impersonal machine, a bureaucracy that, at the factory level, fails to project a sufficiently "human" image. Finally, the very aims of the German labor movement have not been defined explicitly enough.

The German labor movement has never been revolutionary. Before 1914, while the Confédération Générale du Travail was attacking the French Socialist Party for its moderation, German union leaders were exercising a moderating influence within the German Socialist Party. In November, 1918, labor leaders concluded an agreement with management which gave numerous advantages to the workers but which by its very existence demonstrated that the labor movement did not challenge the actual structure of German society. Following World War II, the great ambition of German trade unionists was to realize the notion of comanagement, both at the level of the national economy and at the factory level. The 1951 law, obtained after the DGB threatened a strike, gave only limited satisfaction. Another law passed the following year marked a clear defeat for the DGB, since the sort of comanagement that was now extended throughout German industry no longer put the unions on an equal footing with the owners. Since then, there has been very limited progress and, furthermore, the idea of comanagement has lost much of its appeal: All investigations have demonstrated that the miners and metal-workers, for example, have felt no great material or psychological change in their lives since the introduction of the new system, especially since their *Arbeitsdirektoren* very often acquire the outlook and attitudes of management.

Another idea that was and still is at the heart of the German labor movement is the defense of political democracy in that country. For a time, the DGB was opposed to any German rearmament, and certain of its leaders, as well as members, joined in campaigns against giving West Germany nuclear arms. But the majority has felt that this was a form of political action that was more the responsibility of the political parties than of the unions, especially since union leaders, if not members, have always maintained very close ties with the SDP. Thus, today, the prime goals of trade unionism in West Germany are essentially the classic demands for higher salaries and shorter working hours. In those areas, the record, as presented to the Congress of the DGB in October, 1962, was encouraging. In 1961, 12 million workers and 2.3 million other employees obtained, by means of 14,300 collective-bargaining agreements, wage increases of more than 10 per cent. The 40-hour week will be introduced progressively. (In the metals industry, for example, the work-week was 44 hours in January, 1961; a year later, it was 42.5 hours.) By January, 1964, there was a 41.25-hour work-week, and there should be a 40-hour week by July, 1965.

To achieve these demands, the unions have seldom had

recourse to the strike—for two very different reasons. On the one hand, the unions can dispose of such large strike funds that they have been able to substitute the threat of a strike for the reality, management being well aware that strikers could hold out for quite some time. The metal-workers' strike in Schleswig, which lasted from October 24, 1956, to February 15, 1957, cost the union and the DGB over $7 million: The strikers received more than half their normal salary; a daily four-page paper was published for union members and their families; a huge cultural program was set up to help the days go by, while press conferences, posters, and sound trucks disseminated material designed to create a sympathetic public. More often, however, the union leaders simply obtain a vote in favor of a strike (a majority of 75 per cent of all union members of more than three-months' standing is necessary for this, according to DGB regulations) and then sit down at the bargaining table with this formidable ace up their sleeves.

On the other hand, strikes have become increasingly unpopular, or, more exactly, the unions have increasingly found themselves in a rather weak position. In 1949, the DGB seemed the very incarnation of the political ideals of the new Germany. Today, however, if it is still considered perfectly democratic while fighting Communism, when it denounces the disparities between ideal and reality in the social and economic democracy of West Germany, then the DGB is thought of at best as a spoilsport—at worst, as a traitor. From this point of view, a strike becomes an attack on law and order and economic growth. The attitude of a major newspaper like the *Frankfurter Allgemeine* is charac-teristic of this. When a strike is threatened, the editorialist first reminds his readers that the right to strike constitutes a fundamental liberty, but then goes on to add that in this particular instance, a strike would seriously injure the economy and only serve the interests of the East. The union most often denounced is I.G.-Metall, and its president, Otto Brenner, takes a political stand that is indeed left of the Social Democratic Party.

The fundamental question now facing the DGB is whether to resign itself to being one pressure group among many, whether to cease its efforts to effect any profound transformations in West German society. This is, of course, what the American labor movement has done. But while in America, the Democratic Party, which derives much of its strength from the unions, is often in power, in Germany the more militant German workers have never been represented in the government of the Federal Republic, and the risk is that they will feel increasingly alienated from a state that, ironically, they did much to build. If the DGB cannot retrieve the full confidence of its members and if it is increasingly treated as a second-class power among the forces shaping domestic politics, the workers of West Germany may soon lapse into complete indifference. The resulting weakening of political democracy in that eventuality could very easily be matched by a violent hostility toward the government, should there ever be a major economic recession. This consideration is one of the main arguments in favor of a "great coalition" government including the SPD and CDU after the 1965 elections.

2. The Churches

Among the forces whose influence on public life helps to delineate the particular features of West German democracy, the churches occupy a privileged position. This is due, above all, to their juridical situation. In the United States, membership in a church is a strictly personal matter. In France, also, this is true, and one's religion is not even indicated on public documents. In Germany, where there has never been any formal separation of Church and State, there is hardly a document on which the citizen does not have to state his religion. Every baptized German belongs in theory to some church and is taxed for its support. In order to be absolved of the necessity of paying this tax it is not enough to cease believing in God. One must make an official declaration of having left the Church and obtain the right no longer to pay the *Kirchensteuer*.

A second reason for the influence of the churches in Germany is that in the chaos of 1945 they appeared as the only solid institutions remaining, the only refuge to which people could come and bathe their wounds, material and moral. But at the same time one had to make a searching examination of his conscience, at least in theory. On August 23, 1945, the assembly of German Catholic bishops published a declaration which read in part:

Many Germans, even from our own ranks, allowed themselves to be led astray by the false doctrines of national-socialism; they looked on indifferently while crimes were committed against freedom and human dignity; many, by their attitude, lent assistance to the criminals; many became criminals themselves. A heavy responsibility weighs on those who, by their influence, might have prevented such crimes and who not only failed to exercise that influence but actually helped to make those crimes possible and in so doing declared their solidarity with the criminals.

Seventeen years later, the appeal was renewed. Three weeks before the opening of the Ecumenical Council in 1962, the same Assembly of Fulda declared:

> In this historic hour, we strongly urge all members of our diocese to do deep and solemn penance for all the frightful crimes which have been committed by godless governments, in the name of our people, in violation of fundamental human rights.
>
> In this call for penitence, once again we are especially reminded of the inhuman destruction of the Jewish people, a people which passed on to men the revelation of the one true God and to which, in his flesh, belonged Jesus Christ, the redeemer of the world.

Under the Federal Republic, the Roman Catholic Church of Germany was for the first time no longer a minority faith. The slight numerical difference between Catholics and Protestants in West Germany today is more than compensated for by the lack of structure and cohesion among the Protestant churches. Insofar as one can generalize about national types of Catholicism, one could speak of Catholic Germany as occupying a religious position somewhere between that of France and Spain. This is true whether the point of comparison be the rapport between Church and State, religious toleration, education, the role of the laity within the Church, social problems, anti-Communism, or political intervention. The laity are far more strictly controlled by the Church hierarchy in Germany than in France. But one of the reasons for this is that the German laity have to be stimulated, prodded into taking the initiative, while the French Church may often only have to apply the brakes and channel the activities of its members.

Moreover, neither German Catholics nor their clergy seem in general to make any particular effort to separate that which belongs to God and that which belongs to Caesar. The mixture of being against clerical interference in politics and yet having deep conviction which characterizes the liveliest areas of French Catholicism has no equivalent in West Germany. Once, during a meeting between French and German Catholic journalists, the French participants were divided on every issue but one: They congratulated themselves on their divergent views, insofar as they reflected a kind of political pluralism that stood opposed to the notion of a single, all-embracing Christian Party. In West Germany, however, prevailing Catholic opinion is rather like that in Belgian politics: Differences between Catholics must end in a compromise, if not an actual synthesis, *within* the same party, which will then be able to act from a position of strength in those areas in which the Church has a direct interest—notably in the matter of schools and education.

In addition, German Catholic anti-Communism is not the same as in France, or, rather, it corresponds, on the whole (with a few exceptions), to one well-defined sector of Catholic opinion in France. The German Catholic condemnation of Communism is made not only from a religious and moral basis, but also on the grounds of the supposed excellence of "Western civilization," which permits the believer to close his mind to criticism from the other camp with a good conscience. Yet changes in this attitude do seem to be coming about, as was shown by the positions taken by the German episcopacy during the Ecumenical Council at the end of 1962: Cardinal Frings, Archbishop of Cologne, and Cardinal Liénart, Archbishop of Lille, both intervened at the same time and in the same way to propose what one could describe as a Church open to the modern world and to its problems.

During the Hitler era, German Protestantism was divided between two hostile minority groups—the "German Christians" who were willing instruments of Nazism, and the "Confessing Church," the true communicants of the church who courageously resisted—and an indecisive, malleable majority. After the war, German Protestants set about a complete overhaul of their polity. In August, 1945, the Conference of Treysa decided to change the name of the church, a decision of great significance. Thereafter, there no longer would be an Evangelical German Church incarnating a specifically German type of Protestantism, but an Evangelical Church in Germany—that is to say, a German branch of a world-wide Protestantism. The structural organization of the EKD (*Evangelische Kirche in Deutschland*) was completed in 1948 at Eisenach. The EKD is a federation of twenty-seven autonomous provincial churches (*Landeskirchen*), with, at the head of each, either a bishop (*Landesbischof*) or a president (*Kirchenpräsident*). The EKD represents its member churches before the civil authorities, coordinates their activities, and may take up a stand in the name of German Protestantism —but does not itself, properly speaking, constitute a Church.

At Treysa, a fundamental error of the past had been pointed up in these words: "It was a badly mistaken view of Lutheranism that led us to believe that the only responsibility we bore toward the state was obedience, that it was our duty to preach a Christianity of obedience, that we should shape our religion to the purposes of obedience, at least so long as the state did not ask us to commit a manifest sin." Thereafter, Protestantism was to try to develop among its faithful a sense of civic responsibility, and an awareness of the political, social, and international realities of the contemporary world. In 1945, so-called "Evangelical Academies" were begun; their value and success have been great even though it cannot be said that vigor of thought, independence of spirit, and the courage to face controversial issues squarely have been consistently maintained in all of them. In addition, a lay movement known as the *Kirchentag* was begun, which, like the *Katholikentag*, brings together an enormous mass of the faithful, after their extensive preparation at the parish level.

The *Kirchentag* of 1951, held in Berlin, had as its motto: "We are brothers all the same." There were almost as many East Germans present as West Germans, for the EKD makes no distinction between its members on either side of the Iron Curtain. The Lutheran churches of Hanover and Bavaria are in theory closer to those of Saxony and Thuringia than to those of the Palatinate or Baden. (The Federal Republic has three times the population of East Germany, but, in 1950, 43 per cent of all German Protestants lived east of the Elbe; 80 per cent of the population of East Germany then belonged to the EKD.) The political schism of Germany has therefore been felt deeply by the Evangelical Church in Germany, and its major concern has been to avoid any aggravation of the split.

Quite understandably, the problems of reunification and rearmament have profoundly divided the EKD leadership. On the "neutralist" side, the fight has been led mainly by Pastor Niemöller, Director of the EKD's bureau of foreign affairs until 1955, and by Dr. Heinemann, a former federal

Minister of the Interior and until March, 1955, lay president of the synod of the EKD. Since 1957, the dispute has abated, both because the more "leftist" elements have fallen into a minority position and, above all, because events in East Germany have become increasingly unacceptable to everyone in the West: the efforts to deny the Church to the young people, to stamp out church activities, and to reduce contacts between the two Germanies. Today, East German participation in the *Kirchentage* is virtually nominal. To German Protestantism, then, the Berlin Wall is profoundly significant, and not only as a symbol.

3. The Press and the Intellectuals

As in other countries, the press constitutes an essential element in the makeup of the Federal Republic. As elsewhere also, to the written news has now been added the spoken news and the televised news. The German system of broadcasting is extremely decentralized. Munich, Frankfort, Cologne, Hamburg, Stuttgart, Baden-Baden, and Saarbrücken coordinate their programming but are completely independent of one another. Organized as public utilities, their statute guarantees both their autonomy with regard to the state and their right to give free expression to diverse opinions. One television network is used in common by the various broadcasting organizations, and the second, whose headquarters are in Mainz, is jointly operated by the *Länder*. The system is not perfect, but the freedom of opinion and the variety of social or political subjects discussed on the air are highly commendable.

Newspapers also enjoy a rather enviable position in the Federal Republic. The principal German dailies have a balanced budget and, as opposed to their French or American equivalents, they have a high proportion of subscriptions, the sale of which considerably reduces the costs of distribution, which absorbs virtually all profits of papers that have to be sold by newsboys or on newsstands. The press has always been decentralized in Germany, and today, Berlin's special situation has again diminished the importance of the old capital city. A good number of German cities support one or several worthwhile dailies, each with a good editorial staff and foreign correspondents. On the other hand, the small local papers have such a difficult time that they have resorted to a system of syndicated matrices. Whole pages of the paper are made up of unsigned articles that are written and prepared in central offices, then sent out to the dozens of dailies, often with no staff except the editor himself, who prints them without changing a line, but adding only a few pages of announcements and local news.

Small or large, the majority of these newspapers call themselves independent. Only a few admit they are more or less sympathetic to any particular political group. And these have a difficult time of it financially. The German public wants a press which is "above party politics" (*überparteilich*), and the Socialists, for example, have understood this so well that they far prefer to influence public opinion through papers sympathetic to them (*parteinahe*) than through specifically party organs.

The paper with by far the largest circulation in West Germany is the *Bild-Zeitung*, with a circulation of 3.5 million. Sold at a price very much lower than the other papers, it is the very worst type of sensationalist newspaper, both degraded and degrading. On the other hand, the principal

morning papers refuse to pander to this appetite for scream-
ing headlines and demonstrate a considerable degree of
seriousness and dignity, both in their presentation and their
writing of news and editorials. The space devoted to international news is rather large, and "human interest stories"
do not crowd out the commentaries on local events. Political articles are only rarely inspired by that facile dema-
gogy which appeals to hate or fans delusive hopes. Whether
in opposition, like the *Frankfurter Rundschau*, which is
vigorously alert to any form of neo-nazism, and the aggressive *Die Welt* of Hamburg; or more in support of the government, like the *Frankfurter Allgemeine*, which is trying
to recapture the prestige of the old *Frankfurter Zeitung;* or
liberal and critical, like the *Süddeutsche Zeitung* of Munich,
they all enjoy a great freedom of expression, which is,
however, limited in respect to the taboos weighing on
German political life.

Weekly journals of opinion are rare. The most complete,
as well as the most intelligently critical, is doubtless *Die
Zeit*, published in Hamburg. But the Federal Republic has
no *New Yorker*, *Canard Enchaîné*, or *Punch*. A sheet with
pretentions to being satirical has dared to use the famous
title *Simplicissimus*, but it is in general trivial in content and
vulgar in tone. Political satire is not to be found in the
German press but in the *Kabarette* (where, unlike cabarets
in other countries, one sees real plays with costumes and
sets), and the barbs are all thrown in an entirely undema-
gogic spirit to audiences who are less wealthy and sophisti-
cated than is usually the case in the U.S. or France. On the
other hand, there is no weekly outside of Germany to com-
pare with *Der Spiegel*. Its anonymous articles and long interviews are all written in the same free, casual style that

appears to be perfectly objective but is in fact expertly treacherous. Often in bad faith, but almost always extremely well-informed, it publishes stories that other journals hush up or haven't heard about, spares no one, and manages to give many of its readers an impression of complete intellectual honesty. It has uncovered more than one scandal and denounced more than one contradiction which, without it, would have passed without notice. In a sense, it is the very incarnation of freedom of the press; but the almost complete absence of any constructive commentary, the tone of denunciation that penetrates many of its stories, helps to encourage the public aversion toward all forms of politics.

But even if one may fairly accuse *Der Spiegel* of showing a certain anticonformist conformity (at least until 1963, when the fight against Franz-Josef Strauss seemed to result in an actual "taming" of the newspaper, which is now far less aggressive than it was two years ago), its critical spirit is on the whole refreshing in a country where prosperity has had only too great a tendency to create a rather complacent stuffiness. The intellectuals, who, in times of doubt and in times of new developments, may be in the forefront of events, are almost of necessity outsiders in times of satisfaction and ideological uniformity. In any case, Germany has never, except for a few years during the Weimar Republic, had a place or role for the intellectual such as one finds in France. At all times, the life of the mind and the economic and social life of the country have developed separately. Whether from disdain or ignorance, German intellectuals have always tended to hold themselves aloof from their country's political life; in a philosopher, for example, profound metaphysics might happily co-exist with craven civic pusillanimity. And writers willingly devote their lives to the quest for the *ewig Menschliche* without taking any particular notice of the assuredly transient but also important realities of the world around them. The indifference of the universities, shuttered in their ivory towers of pure learning, contributed not a little to make smooth Hitler's way to power. Whatever one may think of the idea of *engagement* or of the competence (or lack of it) of intellectuals in political affairs, their role in German life is far more limited than that of their American counterparts or than that of their French colleagues, even under the Fifth Republic. They are themselves partly responsible for this; the negativism shown, for instance, by the "Group 47" in Munich cannot but limit their influence. But above all, one can glimpse a movement toward a sort of moral attitude in which the idea of building a *better* order, which dominated German thought immediately after the war, has given way to that of maintaining and defending the present order, even against criticism. The intellectuals must be careful to defend themselves against the accusation that they exercise a corrosive influence; but those who wish to could have a tonic effect on Germany's national life, whether through reviews, press, radio, or television, or again, through a kind of teaching of liberal democracy which constitutes one of the principal tasks that post-Hitlerian Germany has assumed.

VII

The Germans and Their Past

A<small>NY</small> democratic regime to be worthy of the name must be not tolerated and endured, but supported and understood by its citizens. In the Federal Republic, the question of civic responsibility and responsiveness assumed two forms, at once distinct and related. In the first place, it was necessary to persuade the people, particularly young people, to admit the need for their participation in public life; and, in the second place, it was necessary to acknowledge and understand the worst aspects of the Hitlerian era. Though hampered by the seeming permanence of horrible past events and by the apathy induced by prosperity, a remarkable effort has been made, and in general, the results have been most encouraging.

1. A Continuing Effort

The government, unions, churches, youth movements, public universities, press and mass media, all have constantly helped to form, in the minds of thoughtful German people, an understanding of Nazism. In doing so, the situation of the government has been particularly difficult. If it were to do little in this regard, it would be quickly reproached for neglecting to encourage democracy; if it were to do too much, there would soon be talk of government propagandizing. Obviously, the government has not avoided all the dangers of interference, but the aid it gives to youth organizations, for example—aid designed to help their educational projects—is shared in common by these movements themselves. The weekly *Das Parlament*, which gives an impartial and lively view of parliamentary debates and contains supplements on history and contemporary affairs, is controlled by members of the opposition as well as the government. It is published by a remarkable institution called the Central Office for Political Education, which distributes numerous brochures, underwrites longer works, and helps various private educational efforts. Apart from articles designed to give a better understanding of institutions and the citizen's role in the Federal Republic, the basic content of its publications is a mixture of anti-Nazism and anti-Communism. Thanks to this effort, the German opposition to Hitler and the Nazi massacres is better known in Germany. A brochure on the gas chambers, a speech by President Heuss at the unveiling of a memorial at Bergen-Belsen, these and other materials have been widely distributed in the schools, the universities, and the unions.

In fact, "political" or "civic" education has come to be an accepted fact of life almost everywhere in the Federal Republic. Various means (contests, games, etc.) are often employed to render the material more lively. But it is obvious that these programs would be valueless without the good will of the teachers and without texts of good quality. This is as true for the teaching of history as for civic education, and a good portion of the professors take their responsibilities seriously. A school teacher might, for example, replace an hour of drill with an hour of broadcast debate from the *Bundestag*, on which he would then comment. In the area of textbooks, work on a very large scale has already been done. In particular, the International Institute of School Books at Brunschvig has organized a number of bilateral international meetings that have provided texts which are beginning to inspire certain German works.

On the theory that the past must not be forgotten but overcome, books on Nazism and its horrors have followed one another at a great rate, and the distribution of such films as Alain Resnais's *Nuit et Brouillard* has been encouraged. The distribution of *The Diary of Anne Frank*, the efforts of various Jewish-Christian organizations, and increased contacts with Israel have all contributed to the fight against antisemitism and helped to foster that "collective shame"—as opposed to "collective guilt"—which President Heuss used to speak of. Moreover, a collective responsibility, in the sense of a civil responsibility, was accepted by the German-Israeli reparations treaty of September, 1952, which provided that Germany furnish Israel with free merchandise to a total value of 3.45 billion DM. Negotiations on this treaty had been preceded by a declaration in the *Bundestag* by Chancellor Adenauer that "unspeakable crimes have been committed in the name of the German people, crimes that demand of us both material and moral reparations." He received the hearty support of all parliamentary groups and, since 1952, Germany has lived up to her Israeli obligations with exemplary loyalty, especially if one considers the great pressures exerted by the Arab world.

With regard to the role of the army in national life, new legislation has established a number of mechanisms designed to prevent the recurrence of any of the old abuses. Conscientious objectors are respected in a liberal spirit: By August 31, 1963, out of 12,042 cases of people claiming to be conscientious objectors, 9,169 were accepted as such. The parliamentary delegate responsible for the control over and defense of the basic rights of members of the armed forces received from servicemen, in 1961 alone, 4,380 complaints of abuse, of which 1,330 were recognized as completely justified and another 296 as partially justified. The availability to the recruits of this direct appeal to a *Bundestag* delegate made it possible for rapid sanctions to be taken against the few officers or noncoms who were guilty of bullying. (And in 1963, the government acted quickly to punish and to bring to civil trial the officers responsible for the inhuman treatment of recruits at Nagold.) The operation of this system has been helped considerably by the fact that the military establishment enjoys little prestige among the general population.

2. Survivals and Survivors

It would be easy to go on listing examples of efforts and successes proving that the remnants of the past are being rooted out with energy and efficiency. Since this constructive effort is not very spectacular, it is, unfortunately, hardly ever mentioned in the press, above all in the foreign press, whose readers seem to prefer feeling a little shiver of apprehension or burst of indignation in learning of some shocking occurrence.

And in fact, these occurrences have not been lacking in

the Federal Republic. Just as there have been those who have tried to inform themselves of the past, there have been others who are reticent or willfully ignorant. The great majority of teachers avoid mention of the more delicate aspects of their national past and teach no history after the nineteenth century. The older generation of teachers has already been wounded by too many purges, and the younger men in general learn precious little about the immediate past from their university faculties, which, in Germany as elsewhere in Europe, would prefer not to discuss events until they have had the time to ripen in a long silence. In any event, the problem of how to deal with and present to German children the acts of horrible barbarity that were committed in the name of their country is far harder to resolve than non-Germans often seem to feel. In France, for example, what will the textbooks say about the conquest of Algeria in the 1830's or the Algerian war in the 1950's, or in the United States, about the Indians or the discrimination against Negroes?

The rearming of Germany has certainly not facilitated the job of these "teachers of democracy." The reversal of policy was terribly brutal. The first plans for a German contribution to the defense of Europe were being discussed at a time when piloting glider planes and fencing for sport were banned as "militaristic." In 1949, praise was showered on the young Germans who expressed their disgust at the sight of a uniform; they were the model pupils of the accusers. Then, suddenly, they became the accused. On the other hand, the real continuity of thought was found among the anti-Nazis who persevered in their opposition to any totalitarianism, and not among the old nationalists who now feel themselves to be necessary again. And yet, the German sergeant who was asked to prepare to fight the same enemy on the same land could easily believe that it was the same war about to begin all over again. Above all, it was unavoidable that the new *Bundeswehr* would require the services of general officers who, whatever their feelings previously and no matter how carefully they were selected now, had served under Hitler.

Thus did the generals join the whole group of judges, high civil servants, and university professors who should never again have been given posts of responsibility but who now were "indispensable." It is not the occasional sign of neo-nazism that should trouble the careful and objective student of the Federal Republic; the little groups and privately printed publications that attempt a limited apology for the past have laughably little influence. Rather it is the power and prestige in public life of men whose intentions had perhaps been good, who perhaps had tried "to avoid the worst" (but what "worst" was thereby avoided?), who perhaps had only howled along with the other wolves and never took the initiative themselves—the continuance in or return to authority of these men is difficult to justify in a society that does not lack honorable professions. The best-known case in point is that of Dr. Hans Globke, who was secretary of state to the Chancellery under Adenauer until 1963 and a legal consultant for the antisemitic legislation of 1935. Among the judges, the situation is particularly shocking. In July, 1962, a newly appointed attorney general before the Supreme Court had to resign when it was revealed that he had enforced and accelerated the punishment of "asocials" and "enemies of the people." At the same time, there went into effect a law especially voted by Parliament that allowed any judge who wished to retire on pension to do so before a new investigation was made into his past. It was the past history of these judges which explains in great part a whole series of scandalous decisions: the suits brought by Nazi victims thrown out of court on a derisory legal quibble, former Nazi dignitaries awarded comfortable pensions, and so on.

Antisemitism also still exists in the Federal Republic, even though there are hardly any Jews left in Germany. Other components of the national-socialist ideology have also left perceptible traces in textbooks, curriculums, in occasional individual or collective behavior. To the strong desire of many leaders and others to acknowledge the past, there corresponds a less publicized but equally real desire among the average citizen to forget the past and keep silent. Typically, during the Eichmann trial, it was the young people who questioned their parents and brought into German homes the kind of knowledge their parents had never given them. And if, in 1964, the best newspapers gave considerable space to the trial of the Auschwitz criminals, it is certainly not because the general public pressured them to do so.

3. A "Normalized" Future

However, one should not be misled by these unpleasant aspects of the Federal Republic, for there are two factors that today attenuate their importance and may one day eliminate them altogether. The natural aging of the embittered and impenitent condemns them to a slow extinction and no posterity, provided circumstances continue to deny them all possibility of injecting the younger generation with their nostalgia and their rancor. Each year that passes in political stability and economic success constitutes a step toward the definitive elimination of the poisons of the past. Moreover, the social strata from which sprang the mass of Hitler's supporters are in the process of transformation, if not disappearance. The industrial society of the Federal Republic has hardly any place for a *petite bourgeoisie* struggling both against the trusts that threaten to proletarianize it and the "reds" who will defend it but at the cost of dissolving it into the despised masses. With regard to the interplay of political and social forces, and to the problems confronting youth and trade unionism, the Federal Republic has the same advantages and the same difficulties as other countries belonging to the same type of civilization.

The evolution of German youth is characteristic in this respect. The absence of illusions, the refusal to throw around any of "the big words," the fear of commitment, at the same time a healthy realism and a certain serenity— are these traits peculiar to Germany? On the contrary, the majority of the younger generation in the West seems to be neither rebellious nor resigned; they are suspicious of words, not too much interested in politics, and will not be mobilized for any ideal whatsoever. But they are reasonably fond of their work, concerned about raising a family; they easily find distraction in the trivial but not completely despicable things that a technical civilization puts at their disposal. The situation in France, or the United States, is not perhaps so very different. Attitudes toward the past have almost acquired a completely new meaning: It is in terms of a sort of transnational society that Germany seeks to understand the ideology whose poisons do not survive in Germany alone, a Germany, furthermore, whose citizens are easily resigned to see their country reduced to a second-rate power.

VIII

The Federal Republic in
International Life

THE Federal Republic of Germany has been a sovereign
state since 1955. Heavily industrialized and well popu-
lated, West Germany is second among all countries in the
volume of her foreign trade. Yet prestige and power are
matters of small concern to its citizens and government:
Well-being at home is far more important than influence
abroad; the idea of the West is more important than the
idea of the nation; the desire to preserve the freedom of
Berlin and bring freedom to their compatriots in the East
is more important than the possible grandeur of a country
whose very definition is vague.

1. Adenauer's Foreign Policy

In 1949, the first goal of German foreign policy had
necessarily to be the right to have a foreign policy, to cease
being the passive object in international politics and to
become an active participant. The problem was how to
reach this goal. By taking a high-handed approach with the
occupying forces—this was the answer given by the in-

transigent chief of the Social Democratic opposition, Kurt
Schumacher. By inspiring the Allies with confidence
through an irrevocable commitment to their side—this was
the answer of Chancellor Adenauer. He considered it essential to demonstrate suppleness and flexibility as well as to
show that one knew how to give pledges, pledges that
would be largely compensated for by the gains the Allies
would surely grant their new friend, since they would
thereby obtain even further advantage for themselves. In
the particular case of German rearmament, the first step
consisted of a letter from Adenauer suggesting a German
contribution to Western defense. In making the suggestion,
he anticipated what the Americans wanted, and knowingly
counted on the inevitable rapid progress in the direction
of full equality of West Germany's rights. At the same
time, however, he deepened the division between the two
Germanies.

How much did Adenauer's personality affect the outcome of his policies? Abroad, he attracted widespread
admiration, which redounded to the benefit of his country.
He was thought of as the incarnation of a Germany one
could have confidence in, at once dependable and virtuous.
Men of otherwise widely differing opinions paid homage
to Germany in the person of its Chancellor. From John
Foster Dulles to Antoine Pinay, from the socialist Spaak
to the liberal Salvador de Madariaga, from Pierre Mendès-
France to General de Gaulle—all expressed their hopes that
the Federal Republic would remain for as long as possible
the Germany of Adenauer. His countrymen were grateful
for his attracting admiration. A very effective poster in
the 1953 electoral campaign announced: "He has re-estab-
lished our ties with the free world."

Abroad, there was much speculation that after Adenauer's departure the door would open to all kinds of trouble, but this was to misunderstand the givens of the situation. Why should a Germany without Adenauer go downhill? To be sure, the Chancellor showed himself particularly tenacious and unshakeable. But would he have been this way if feelings of anti-Communism, born of the sufferings of the war and postwar period, nourished by the nearness of the other, totalitarian Germany, and also by twelve years of Hitlerian propaganda—if these feelings were not deeply rooted in the great majority of his fellow citizens? In France (as in America and, especially, Great Britain), a sort of permanent suspicion often prevents commentators from understanding the fundamental element of the German situation. When the Germans refuse to negotiate with the East, they become "warmongers." But when they do negotiate, they raise the ghost of Rapallo and the treaty of August, 1939. In reality, the vast majority of the West Germans have made a choice that is exceptional in the twentieth century. They have preferred to maintain certain forms in their political and economic society rather than strive after national unity. Between reunification, bringing with it the danger of a "Communized" reunited Germany, and the absence of reunification, bringing with it the certainty that West Germany will preserve its liberties, the people have clearly opted for the second.

This situation and the whole tenor of public opinion therefore severely limits any freedom of choice between fundamental options. However, Adenauer made certain decisions and adopted certain attitudes that were not necessarily implied in the options open to him. Examples of this would be the decisions on rearmament, the *rapprochement* with France (especially under the Fifth Republic), and the commitment to the Common Market. Even if these decisions were of arguable merit, Adenauer has shown that he possesses the greatest quality of the statesman, the ability to distinguish between what is essential and what is secondary and not to be diverted by considerations of purely ephemeral importance from a basic orientation. Either because his policies were the best possible ones (as he would claim) or because he created irreversible situations (as his opponents claim), Adenauer was able to rally the opposition to his foreign policy. After having denounced the Schuman Plan of 1950 as a catastrophe for Germany, the SPD ended by voting for the Rome treaties creating Euratom and the Common Market; after having launched a great *Deutschlandplan* in 1959 that involved a vast change of policy, the SPD officially abandoned it the following year. It is true, however, that European politics are today more uncertain than in the past and the lack of clarity in German reunification policy renders very difficult the definition of any real change of over-all policy.

2. Which Europe?

The notion of a somehow united Europe was immediately popular in Germany. It was natural that the Federal Republic should be more "European" than France, herself more "European" than Great Britain. Germany was well aware of the total disaster that had been the result of her nationalism; France knew that she had been victorious only through the intervention of other powers, but that the war had not profoundly shaken her national institutions; Great Britain knew that she was saved in 1940 only by a sudden quickening of national pride. Yet European sentiment in Germany has never been all of a piece. At the extremes one finds the enthusiasts and the cynics. The first group is mostly recruited from among the young, and their sincere idealism for a long time mobilized a great many young people in the services of Europe. Their zeal made them persistent, but their sentimental impatience has not always been a good defense against the inevitable disappointments. Neither have they always been able to see that it is much easier to renounce rights and prerogatives not yet regained (as Germany has done) than voluntarily to give up powers that have not yet been lost (as Germany asked its partners to do). For the cynics, however, Europe was first and foremost the best means for Germany to attain full equality of rights among the nations. Once this equality had been gained, Europe lost much of its appeal. Between these two extremes, there were and are a mass of Germans of the most diverse motivation.

The wish to achieve some sort of political integration, at least at the level of a common political organization capable of acting on majority decision—this remains the preeminent hope of most Germans, even though many do not fully realize the consequence of such an integration. For example, what German government could bind itself to follow a decision contrary to its views on a question such as East Germany? Nonetheless, West Germans are wont to fret about France's reticence in discussing political integration. At the same time, though in the opposite direction, the Common Market has given rise to at least two kinds of doubt in Germany as well. On the one hand, industrialists and unionists share Erhard's fears about the effects of the Common Market on Germany's foreign trade. For trade

with countries outside the Common Market is more important for Germany than for France. Germany did not
want a liberalization of trade within the Common Market
if it were accompanied by protectionism with regard to
Scandinavia and Great Britain. On the other hand, the
EEC, in the spirit of its creators, should be something far
more than a mere free-trade zone; its goals are a common
economic policy, common planning, and common action.
Yet until 1961, one could say that French business was
more taken with the notion of planning than the Social
Democrats were in Germany.

The desire not to sacrifice relations with Great Britain
to a sort of exclusive friendship with France is almost unanimous in West Germany, and this despite General de
Gaulle's spectacular success during his trip to Germany in
September, 1962. Nevertheless, relations with France have
become far closer than those with any other country, not
only at the governmental level but also through the establishment of permanent contacts among social groups and
between the most diverse sectors in public life. But
neither Social Democrats nor Free Democrats, nor men like
Schröder and the new generation of the CDU want to see
Europe dominated by a Franco-German alliance. They
feel this way primarily because the solidarity of the West
is more important to them than the autonomy of Europe,
and because General de Gaulle's nationalism is rather
troubling. They also deeply resented France's brutal ex-
clusion of England from the Common Market in 1963.

For these reasons, the Franco-German Treaty of January
22, 1963, was not greeted with much enthusiasm in the
Federal Republic. It was not the principle of close cooperation with another country that was at issue. On cultural,

scientific, and other matters, many of the provisions of the treaty went far in the direction pointed out by those who began the contacts and exchanges between France and Germany immediately after the war. But on either side of the frontier, qualified observers feared that the whole program, though strongly encouraged by the treaty, might appear to the public to be slightly tinged with the politics of the moment. For the German leaders, the treaty was valuable only to the degree that it might somehow serve as a model and nucleus for a multilateral cooperation between the various countries in a Europe moving toward egalitarian unity.

With or without Britain, with a planned economy or a free market economy, what are the responsibilities of a prosperous Europe toward the underdeveloped countries of the world? With regard to Africa and Asia, the awareness of a job to be done has only very slowly been felt in Germany. The reason, again, may be that the task of "re-education" accomplished by the Allies was here, as in the matter of rearmament, more successful than appeared desirable several years later. With no more nationalistic ambitions, no more involvement in world affairs, the Germans would be content to raise their standard of living and do business. Furthermore, the hardening of minds in the resistance to Communism in Europe gave Germany a fairly good conscience: They are firm on the Berlin question; in this way, they make their contribution to the efforts of the Western bloc. That the main battlefield in the struggle between the two camps is the uncommitted world seems to have penetrated but slowly into the minds of most Germans. A positive development has been noticeable recently, however, first on the level of government leadership, then in public opinion. In June, 1962, a poll was taken on the question, "Is it or is it not fair that the Federal Republic should contribute to help the developing countries of Africa, Asia, and Latin America?" Forty-six per cent of the respondents answered in the affirmative, 36 per cent in the negative. And whereas for the period 1950–56 German foreign aid amounted to only 2.5 billion DM, it was 2.6 billion for the single year 1960, and 3.2 billion in 1961.

3. The Oder-Neisse Line, Berlin, and the D.D.R.

If German aid to Africa and Asia continues to develop, the major foreign concern of the country still remains, of course, the fate of those parts of Germany outside the Federal Republic. Among these, should one count the territories situated east of the Oder-Neisse line? They still figure on all German maps, in the textbooks as well as in the railway cars. In official jargon, the D.D.R. is referred to as Middle Germany (*Mitteldeutschland*), thus signalling the fact that Germany does not end at the Oder River. On this subject there is no lack of legal and moral argument, and the emotional and sentimental factors must not be underestimated either. France was close to civil war over the fate of a million non-Arab Algerians, their compatriots. But unlike Algiers and Oran, the cities in the D.D.R. are purely European and many of them, like Breslau (today Wroclaw), have been German for much longer than Algeria was French.

But the analogy with the Algerian problem can be extended in another way: The definite nature of the frontier represents in German politics a taboo similar to the taboo about Algerian independence in French politics until 1962;

ministers and party leaders privately recognize the ineluct-
able character of developments, but they will hardly risk
political suicide by going against public opinion on the
matter. For the allies of the Federal Republic, the problem
of reunification concerns the Germany up to but no farther
than the Oder-Neisse line. If, with the exception of General
de Gaulle, they have not admitted it openly, it is to spare
the feelings of the German government, as well as not to
throw away a good bargaining point in any future negotiations with the Soviets. But they are all well aware that any
new modification of the frontier would inevitably bring
into being new waves of refugees and new suffering, and
that Poland today really does extend to the Oder.

On the other hand, there is real unanimity of purpose
behind the German determination and the Western desire
to defend the freedom of those Berliners who have not yet
lost it. The geographically absurd situation of West Berlin
does not prevent the city from having great symbolic value:
its absorption by the East against the constantly reaffirmed
will of its citizens would constitute so crushing a defeat
for the principles claimed by the West that no one any-
where in the world would any longer believe in its guarantee.

But the maintenance of the freedom of the Berliners,
which depends particularly on free access to the city, is
linked to another problem, that of the legal status of the
other Germany. In 1955, the Soviet Union recognized the
Federal Republic, but for the West there has only been
but one German state. Their position has remained the
same ever since the Franco-British-American declaration
of October 3, 1954: "They consider the government of the
Federal Republic as the only German government freely

and legitimately constituted, and therefore capable of speaking in the name of Germany as the representative of the whole German people."

The word "legitimately" is open to argument. If it is a matter of the delegation of sovereignty effected by the Allies, then three of them have as much or as little right as the fourth to grant to "their" Germany the individual sovereignty they had held since June 5, 1945. If it is a question of the legitimacy born of free elections, then a principle is involved that the Western powers do not everywhere act upon with the same degree of commitment, since they maintain ambassadors in both Madrid and Budapest. But the real issue here is, in fact, one of not wanting to give any sort of official consecration to a regime that was obliged to restrain a workers' revolt of June 17, 1953, by force, and that has had to use a wall, barbed wire, observation towers, and machine guns to prevent a mass exodus of its own citizens. Nonetheless, the D.D.R. does exist and the fact is a source of embarrassment for the West, above all for the Federal Republic—whether it is a question of Berlin, relations with uncommitted countries, or the representation of Germany in the Olympic Games. The truth that the Federal Republic must come to terms with, but that it largely refuses to face up to, is the ever more assured place of the Deutsche Demokratische Republik on the international scene.

Relations between the two Germanies also require that the Federal Republic make some formidable choices. In 1962, the East German government asked for economic aid. To grant the request would have been to strengthen a regime that, in the eyes of the vast majority of Germans, represents what the "collaborators" in Paris in 1943 represented to the French; but to refuse it would be to inflict hardship on 17 million compatriots. And since the agreement of December 17, 1963, that opened the Berlin Wall for West Berliners to visit their families during Christmas, there have been discussions among West German leaders about how far one can go in "technical" recognition of the East German authorities, in exchange for some sheerly humanitarian gestures. Little by little, the theme of reunification has passed into the background in relation to the demand for a re-establishment of freedom in the other Germany. But the Federal Republic has not yet asked itself this crucial question: If an international agreement should at once confirm the existence of two German states, secure a liberalization of the regime of the D.D.R., and make contacts between the two easier, would the Federal Republic then renounce the goal of reunification?

4. *A Powerless Power?*

For many long years, people have discussed the chances for German reunification and the means for achieving it. Some Germans, Adenauer being one, were slowly convinced that the extension of the Federal Republic to the Oder River and reunification by absorption were vain hopes. Others, including the Social Democrats, finally recognized that a solution that would detach the Federal Republic from the West and the D.D.R. from the East would be as unacceptable for the one as the other.

One comes, therefore, to a bitter realization: In an era that seems dominated by the idea of self-determination of peoples, 17 million Germans must be deprived of the application of that principle. In what, then, can the policy of the Federal Republic consist, if not in constantly reiterating a demand, and constantly keeping in mind—embarrassing as this is even to its closest allies—an apparently irremediable situation?

Fourteen years after its creation, therefore, the Federal Republic constitutes a paradoxical political reality. From one point of view, it is a regime that functions fairly smoothly and efficiently, a peaceful and prosperous society, a respected partner in the Western camp, one of the strongest economic powers in the modern world. But from another point of view, this great power, this rich and respected country, finds itself utterly powerless to solve its most urgent national problem, a problem that is as much human as political. Born of the division of the world and strengthened by it, the Federal Republic knows that this division is the chief obstacle to its desire to see all Germans reunited. Its new strength and independence do not prevent it from being more dependent on its relations with the truly great powers than many other weaker and apparently less free countries.

A Selected Bibliography

Caught between the necessity of keeping this bibliography reasonably short and the desire to list as many as possible of the most interesting recent titles, I have decided on the following course: Except for a few important books that appeared before 1960, particularly in English, I have cited only the more recent titles which postdate the extensive critical bibliography supplied in my *La Démocratie de Bonn, 1949–1957* (Paris: Armand Colin, 1958) and in the revised and enlarged German edition of the same book, *Die Bonner Demokratie* (Düsseldorf: Rauch, 1960).

Current Material on Current Events in Germany

The daily *Bulletin des Presse- und Informationsamts der Bundesregierung* gives all the principal documents and official communiqués of the Federal Republic, as well as a great deal of statistical information, but its foreign-language editions are of little value. The excellent weekly *Das Parlament*, published by the Central Office for Political Education, spares one the job of going back to the full texts of the parliamentary debates; the periodical *Wirtschaft und*

Statistik with its statistics and analyses, well fills out the material offered in the yearly *Statistisches Jahrbuch*—these latter two both published by the Federal Statistical Office. There are two monthlies devoted entirely to politics—one published in Bonn, *Die politische Meinung* (with a CDU slant); the other in Munich, under the auspices of the Munich School for Political Sciences, *Politische Studien.* Interesting articles can also be found in *Politische Viertel-jahresschrift*, the journal of the German Political Science Association (Cologne); *Der Monat* (Berlin), the German equivalent of *Encounter* or *Preuves; Frankfurter Hefte*, which is a left-of-center Catholic paper; and *Die Neue Gesellschaft* (Cologne), a left-wing socialist organ. In international affairs, there is *Aussenpolitik* (Stuttgart), but the most significant publication in the field is the twice-monthly *Europa-Archiv* (Frankfort), which includes not only extremely interesting articles, but also all the documents and a full chronology concerning current foreign-policy developments. Two French bi-monthlies specialize in German affairs: *Documents*, published by the Bureau International de Liaison et de Documentation in Cologne; and *Allemagne*, the information bulletin of the French Committee for Exchanges with the New Germany, which has a good column on German books.

Occupied Germany

Two remarkable over-all surveys permit the reader to place the "German problem" of the postwar era in perspective: LUDWIG DEHIO, trans. Dieter Pevsner, *Germany and World Politics in the Twentieth Century* (New York: Knopf; London: Chatto and Windus, 1959, 141 pp.); and,

especially, GOLO MANN, *Deutsche Geschichte des neun-
zehnten und zwanzigsten Jahrhunderts* (Frankfort: Fischer,
1958, 989 pp.). A clear and precise view of the period
1919–55 can also be found in the contributions by A.
SCHWARZ, W. HOFER, H. MICHAELIS, and E. DEUERLEIN
in LEO JUST, ed., *Handbuch der deutschen Geschichte*
(Constance: Akademische Verlagsanstalt Athenaion, 1958–
64), the bibliography of which is well supplemented and
completed by INTER NATIONES, ed., *Schrifttum über
Deutschland, 1918–1962: Ausgewählte Bibliographie deutscher Publikationen* (Wiesbaden: Steiner, 1962, 306 pp.).

A historical account of relations between the Allied
powers and of the nature and life of occupied Germany is
provided in ALFRED GROSSER, trans. Richard Rees, *The
Colossus Again: Western Germany From Defeat to Rearmament* (New York: Praeger, 1955, 249 pp.), to which
one might add JOHN L. SNELL, *The Wartime Origins of
the East-West Dilemma Over Germany* (New Orleans:
Hauser, 1959, 268 pp.); HAROLD ZINK, *The United States
in Germany, 1944–1945* (Princeton: Van Nostrand, 1957,
374 pp.); FRANK ROY WILLIS, *The French in Germany,
1945–1949* (Stanford: Stanford University Press, 1962, 308
pp.); and, above all, a remarkable study by JOHN GIMBEL,
*A German Community Under American Occupation: Mar-
burg, 1945–52* (Stanford: Stanford University Press, 1961,
259 pp.), which wisely illuminates how the problems of
the occupation affected and were defined by the Germans
themselves. Mr. Gimbel also provides an excellent discussion of denazification, while the bringing to justice of war
criminals is well presented in ROBERT K. WOETZEL, *The
Nuremberg Trials in International Law* (New York:
Praeger; London: Stevens, 1962, 317 pp.). The life of an

"occupied" people is described by the present editor-in-chief of *Die Zeit*, JOSEF MUELLER-MAREIN, in *Deutschland im Jahre I: Panorama, 1946–1948* (Hamburg: Nannen, 1960, 340 pp.). On the expulsion and transfer of Germans east of the Oder-Neisse, there is JOSEPH B. SCHECHTMAN, *Postwar Population Transfers in Europe, 1945–1955* (Philadelphia: University of Pennsylvania Press, 1962, 417 pp.), but a very moving account, which met with enormous success in Germany, is particularly noteworthy—HANS GRAF VON LEHNDORFF, *Ostpreussisches Tagebuch: Aufzeichnungen eines Arztes aus den Jahren 1945–1947** (Munich: Biederstein, 1961, 308 pp.). The English translation of this book, by Elizabeth Mayer, is entitled *Token of a Covenant* (Chicago, Ill.: Henry Regnery, 1964).

Political Institutions

Two excellent works explain how the Federal Republic was founded: PETER H. MERKL, *The Origin of the West German Republic* (New York: Oxford University Press, 1963, 269 pp.), and JOHN F. GOLAY, *The Founding of the Federal Republic of Germany* (Chicago: University of Chicago Press, 1958, 299 pp.), the latter written by the former Secretary to the Allied High Commission. I should also mention FRIEDRICH KARL FROMME's intelligent study, *Von der Weimarer Verfassung zum Bonner Grundgesetz: Die verfassungspolitischen Folgerungen des parlamentarischen Rates aus Weimarer Republik und nationalsozialistischer Diktatur* (Tübingen: J. C. B. Mohr, 1960, 243 pp.). For all research in primary sources, the essential book is HANS SCHNEIDER, ed., *Bibliographie zum öffentlichen Recht in der Bundesrepublik Deutschland* (Munich, Berlin: C. H. Beck, 1960, 112 pp.).

The study of German political institutions should begin with a reading of at least the first, and preferably both, of the two volumes by THOMAS ELLWEIN, *Das Regierungssystem der Bundesrepublik Deutschland:* Vol. I., *Leitfaden;* Vol. II, *Quellenbuch* (Cologne: Westdeutscher Verlag, 1963, 630 pp.), which offer all the important texts concerning the press, political parties and other groups, electoral laws, procedures of parliamentary groups and of the *Bundestag,* the workings of the government, etc. There is also the ambitious and difficult study by RUDOLF WILDENMANN, *Macht und Konsens als Problem der Innen- und Aussenpolitik* (Frankfort, Bonn: Athenäum, 1963, 364 pp.), which the author himself describes as *Untersuchung des Regierungssystems der Bundesrepublik Deutschland und seine internationale Verflechtung.* For an account of the developments and problems of recent years, there are two collections of essays, the first by one of Germany's best political journalists, the other by a professor of political science who is a journalist as well: FRITZ RENÉ ALLEMANN, *Zwischen Stabilität und Krise: Etappen der deutschen Politik, 1955–1963* (Munich: Piper, 1963, 309 pp.), and THEODOR ESCHENBURG, *Institutionelle Sorgen in der Bundesrepublik: Politische Aufsätze, 1957–1961* (Stuttgart: Schwab, 1961, 279 pp.). Lastly, when Adenauer resigned from the Chancellorship, the government produced a long compendium of his accomplishments in a variety of fields: PRESSE- UND INFORMATIONSAMT DER BUNDESREGIERUNG, *Regierung Adenauer, 1949–1963* (Wiesbaden: Steiner, 1963, 984 pp.).

For the federal aspect of the West German state, there is HANS SCHÄFFER, *Probleme einer Neugliederung des Bundesgebietes* (Berlin: de Gruyter, 1963, 31 pp.), and EDWARD

PINNEY, *Federalism, Bureaucracy, and Party Politics in Western Germany* (Chapel Hill: University of North Carolina Press, 1963, 268 pp.), whose subtitle, "The Role of the Bundesrat," corresponds more nearly to the actual contents of the book. The best way to understand the role of the Federal Constitutional Court is to read the account it has provided of itself, *Das Bundesverfassungsgericht* (Karlsruhe: Müller, 1963, 338 pp.). For an appreciation of the real function of the *Bundestag*, there should be, ideally, supplemental volumes on 1955–57 and 1957–61 to the excellent book by W. KRALEWSKI and K. NEUNREITHER, *Oppositionnelles Verhalten im ersten deutschen Bundestag* (Cologne: Westdeutscher Verlag, 1963, 288 pp.).

Erhard's assumption of power has in no way diminished or rendered out of date an exceptionally valuable book which is noteworthy for both its political and juridical analysis, JEAN AMPHOUX, *Le Chancelier fédéral dans le régime constitutionnel de la République fédérale d'Allemagne* (Paris: Librairie générale de droit et de jurisprudence, 1962, 562 pp.). But there is still no genuinely serious biography of West Germany's first Chancellor. PAUL WEYMAR's book, *Adenauer, his authorized biography* (New York: Dutton; London: Deutsch, 1957), despite its wealth of documentation, is too hagiographic. To the hasty but nevertheless useful works by OTTO KOPP, *Adenauer: Eine biographische und politische Dokumentation* (Stuttgart: Seewald, rev. ed., 1963, 184 pp.), and FRANZ RODENS, *Konrad Adenauer: Der Mensch und der Politiker* (Munich: Knaur, 1963, 142 pp.), there are three books that are preferable: a collection of material gathered in public-opinion polls, E. P. NEUMANN and E. NOELLE, *Umfragen über Adenauer: Ein Porträt in Zahlen* (Bonn: Verlag fur

Demoskopie, 1961, 159 pp.); or, even better, WALTHER FREIBURGER, ed., *Konrad, Bleibst du jetzt zu Haus? Adenauer in der Karikatur* (Oldenburg/Hamburg: Stalling, 1963, 112 pp.), a sequel to *Konrad, sprach die Frau Mama* (1955); or even the book of photographs, BERTRAM OTTO, *Konrad Adenauer und seine Zeit* (Bonn: Berto, 1963, 201 pp.). For a good description of Germany's leading politicians, see the profiles that appeared in the *Frankfurter Allgemeine*, collected in WALTER HENKELS, *99 Bonner Köpfe* (Düsseldorf: Econ, 1963, 330 pp.).

Elections and Party Politics

On the electoral system and the various problems posed in the elections there is HELMUT KOCH, *Wie wird der Bundestag gewählt?* (Bonn: Deutscher Bundes-Verlag, rev. ed., 1961, 86 pp.). UWE W. KITZINGER, *German Electoral Politics: A Study of the 1957 Campaign* (Oxford: Clarendon Press, 1960, 366 pp.), a particularly brilliant work that deserves a wide public, is written by England's foremost specialist on German affairs. There are also ERWIN FAUL, ed., *Wahlen und Wähler in Westdeutschland* (Villingen/Schwarzwald: Ring, 1960, 371 pp.), a collection of on the whole fairly interesting essays; K. KAUFMANN, H. KOHL, and P. MOLT, *Die Auswahl der Bundestagskandidaten 1957 in zwei Bundesländern* (Cologne: Kiepenheuer & Witsch, 1961, 244 pp.), which takes up an essential question that is virtually (and wrongly) ignored by European political scientists; and WERNER W. GRUNDMANN, *Die Rathausparteien: Die rechtliche und faktische Stellung örtlich begrenzter Wählerorganisationen bei den Kommunalwahlen* (Göttingen: Schwartz, 1960, 114 pp.).

The short but substantial book by HELGA GREBING, *Geschichte der deutschen Parteien* (Wiesbaden: Steiner, 1962, 184 pp.), is an excellent historical introduction, but for further study of the postwar political parties, it is essential to consult OSSIP K. FLECHTHEIM, *Dokumente zur parteipolitischen Entwicklung in Deutschland seit 1945* (Berlin: Wendler, 1962–63, 3 vols., 576, 511, 500 pp.), for nowhere else can one find all the necessary documents so intelligently classified and arranged. Among the most important and serious questions that confront the political parties, two have been thoroughly, if somewhat optimistically, studied (particularly the second) in ULRICH DÜBBER, *Parteifinanzierung in Deutschland* (Cologne: Westdeutscher Verlag, 1962, 98 pp.), and ULRICH LOHMAR, *Innerparteiliche Demokratie* (Stuttgart: Enke, 1963, 146 pp.).

The literature on the two largest parties is somewhat deceiving: ARNOLD HEIDENHEIMER, *Adenauer and the CDU: The Rise of the Leader and the Integration of the Party* (The Hague: Nijhoff, 1960, 259 pp.), while serious and solid, nevertheless does not fully utilize the documentation to which the author had access. There is also RAINER BARZEL, ed., *Karl Arnold: Grundlegung christlich-demokratischer Politik in Deutschland: Eine Dokumentation* (Bonn: Berto, 1960, 249 pp.), a cautious compendium of statements by the late leader of the left wing of the CDU. The centenary of the SPD was celebrated with the publication of several useful, if hardly critical, studies—among them, F. OSTERROTH and D. SCHUSTER, *Chronik der deutschen Sozialdemokratie* (Hanover: Dietz, 1963, 672 pp.), and GEORG ECKERT, ed., *1863–1963: Hundert Jahre deutsche Sozialdemokratie: Bilder und Dokumente* (Hanover: Dietz, 1963, unpaginated). The material in the three volumes of A. SCHOLZ and W. OSCHILEWSKI, eds., *Turmwächter der Demokratie: Ein Lebensbild von Kurt Schumacher* (Berlin: Arani, 1952–54), is filled out by KURT SCHUMACHER, *Reden und Schriften* (Berlin: Arani, 1962, 549 pp.). These books do not, however, measure up as the kind of serious study that is so well exemplified by LEWIS EDINGER, *German Exile Politics: The Social Democratic Executive Committee in the Nazi Era* (Berkeley: University of California Press, 1956, 329 pp.). Another important contribution is WILLY BRANDT's autobiography, as told to Leo Landia (pseud.), *My Road to Berlin* (Garden City: Doubleday, 1960, 287 pp.). As for the present political configuration, there are pamphlets such as *Katholik und Godesberger Programm: Zur Situation nach Mater et Magistra* (Bonn: Vorstand der SPD, 1962, 52 pp.), or WILLI EICHLER, *Grundwerte und Grundforderungen im Godesberger Grundsatzprogramm der SPD* (Bonn: Vorstand der SPD, 1962, 24 pp.). The SPD is attacked from the right in ALBRECHT BECKEL and GÜNTHER TRIESCH, *Wohin steuert die SPD?* (Osnabrück: Fromm, 1961, 104 pp.), and questioned as to its very program and platform in MANFRED FRIEDRICH's thoughtful and intelligent *Opposition ohne Alternative? Über die Lage der parlamentarischen Opposition im Wohlfahrtsstaat* (Cologne: Verlag Wirtschaft und Politik, 1962, 109 pp.), and in HORST KRÜGER, ed., *Was ist heute Links?* (Munich: List, 1961, 160 pp.), which is a selection of essays primarily by "left-wing intellectuals."

The interesting but biased documentary selection in H. WEBER, ed., *Der deutsche Kommunismus* (Cologne: Kiepenheuer & Witsch, 1963, 679 pp.), does not take into account the genuine and serious history of the KPD. At the opposite end of the spectrum, the tendencies of the extreme right are well analyzed in MANFRED JENKE, *Verschwörung von rechts? Ein Bericht über den Rechtsradikalismus in Deutschland nach 1945* (Berlin: Colloquium, 1961, 492 pp.), and in HANS HELMUTH KNUETTER, *Ideologien des Rechtsradikalismus im Nachkriegsdeutschland* (Bonn: Röhrscheid, 1961, 230 pp.).

The Ideology of Prosperity

No one work has yet superseded the brilliant study by H. C. WALLICH, *Mainsprings of the German Revival* (New Haven: Yale University Press, 1955, 402 pp.). The articles and speeches in LUDWIG ERHARD, trans. J. A. Arengo-Jones and D. J. S. Thompson, *The Economics of Success* (Princeton: Van Nostrand; London: Thames and Hudson, 1963, 412 pp.), give a clear idea of present governmental policy. There are excellent analyses of German economics and geographic economics in HEINZ KÖNIG, ed., *Wandlungen der Wirtschaftsstruktur in der Bundesrepublik Deutschland* (Berlin: Duncker & Humblot, 1962, 620 pp.). But perhaps the most useful, best prepared, and most readable volume is that of HANS HERBERT GÖTZ, *Weil alle besser leben wollen . . . Porträt der deutschen Wirtschaftspolitik* (Düsseldorf: Econ, 1963, 408 pp.), which, in addition to an excellent over-all survey of the political economy since 1948, contains a helpful chronology of legislation on economic affairs and a very well presented and systematic bibliography.

On the integration of the refugees in West German life, no study has yet appeared to add, from a more critical view-

point, to the wealth of material provided by EUGEN LEM-
BERG and FRIEDRICH EDDING in *Die Vertriebenen in West-
deutschland: Ihre Eingliederung und ihr Einfluss auf
Gesellschaft, Wirtschaft, Politik, und Geistesleben* (Kiel:
Hirt, 1959, 3 vols., 694, 557, 684 pp.).

On the men who control German industry, see—among
the many works by the same author—KURT PRITZKOLEIT,
*Männer, Mächte, Monopole: Hinter den Türen der west-
deutschen Wirtschaft* (Düsseldorf: Rauch, 2nd ed., aug-
mented, 1960, 648 pp.). If, in reading the over-indulgent
GORDON YOUNG, *The Fall and Rise of Alfried Krupp*
(London: Cassell, 178 pp.), or, even more, the veritable
apologia by LOUIS LOCHNER, *Tycoons and Tyrant: German
Industry from Hitler to Adenauer* (Chicago: Regnery,
1954), one feels a certain compassion for the fate of some
of Germany's industrial barons, there are a number of
studies to correct one's impressions of their history, notably
JOSIAH E. DUBOIS, *Generals in Grey Suits* (London: Bodley
Head, 1953, 374 pp.), on the relation between I.-G. Farben
and Auschwitz, and also the revealing and rarely cited J. S.
MARTIN, *All Honorable Men* (Boston: Little, Brown, 1950,
326 pp.), which shows why the tycoons happened to survive Hitler and the occupation.

The principles and the actual legislation of codetermination, and the labor unions' role in preparing and operating
that system, are discussed from many different angles in
different books, notably by ABRAHAM SCHUMAN, *Codetermination: Labor's Middle Way in Germany* (Washington:
Public Affairs Press, 1957, 247 pp.), by HERBERT SPIRO,
The Politics of German Codetermination (Cambridge:
Harvard University Press, 1958, 180 pp.), and by XAVIER
HERLIN, *Les Expériences allemandes de cogestion: Tech-

niques et réalisations (Paris: Librairie Dalloz, 2nd ed., 1960, 282 pp.). But to appreciate the results of the experiment, analyses such as HARDEY WAGNER, *Erfahrungen mit dem Betriebsverfassungsgezetz* (Cologne: Bund Verlag, 1960, 160 pp.), and E. POTTHOF, O. BLUME, and H. DUVERNEL, *Zwischenbilanz der Mitbestimmung* (Tübingen: J .C. B. Mohr, 1961, 371 pp.), are useful.

But it would be a mistake to concentrate solely on the working class in a society in which the white-collar workers are an increasingly important sector of society—see, for instance, LUDWIG NEUNDÖRFER, *Die Angestellten: Neuer Versuch einer Standortbestimmung* (Stuttgart: Enke, 1961, 160 pp.), and HANS BAYER, ed., *Der Angestellte zwischen Arbeiterschaft und Management* (Berlin: Dunker & Humblot, 1961, 468 pp.), or MARIANNE FEUERSENGER, ed., *Gibt es noch ein Proletariat?* (Frankfurt: Europäische Verlagsanstalt, 1962, 99 pp.), whose contributors pose all the basic questions.

The Social and Moral Order

Whether or not the working class does exist as a class in West Germany, the unions constitute an important force, a force of which the two best analyses on the subject are extremely critical. GÜNTER TRIESCH, in *Die Macht der Funktionäre: Macht und Verantwortung der Funktionäre* (Düsseldorf: Rauch, 1956, 480 pp.), minces no words in a description of the unions from the point of view of their paternalism, while THEO PIRKER, in *Die blinde Macht: Die Gewerkschaftsbewegung in Deutschland* (Munich: Mercator, 1960, 2 vols., 320, 338 pp.), traces the unions' postwar history from the point of view one would expect in a man who was expelled from the Economic Research Institute of the DGB for being "too left-wing." To both these remarkable books, one should add WOLFGANG HIRSCH-WEBER, *Gewerkschaften in der Politik, von der Massenstreikdebatte bis zum Kampf um das Mitbestimmungsrecht* (Cologne: Westdeutscher Verlag, 1959, 170 pp.), a more thoughtful treatment, if more limited in its objectives. The basic question Hirsch-Weber asks—What is a political strike?—is examined from all the legal aspects by BERND RÜTTERS, *Streik und Verfassung* (Cologne: Bund Verlag, 1960, 147 pp.). A not unimportant factor, that of labor's role in political education, is discussed by GERHARD WUTHE, *Gewerkschaften und politische Bildung* (Hanover: Verlag für Literatur und Zeitgeschichte, 1962, 312 pp.).

Literature on the German churches and their influence is abundant but incomplete. The forty statements gathered in H. SCHULTZ, ed., *Kritik an der Kirche* (Stuttgart: Kreuz Verlag, 1958, 336 pp.), constitute a good introduction to the problem. Scholars have not clarified the role and behavior of church-goers and believers, but DIETRICH GOLDSCHMIDT, FRANZ STEINER, and HELMUT SCHELSKY, *Soziologie der Kirchengemeinde* (Stuttgart: Enke, 1960, 256 pp.), and R. KOESTER, *Die Kirchentreuen* (Stuttgart: Enke, 1959, 117 pp.), make a number of useful observations. Among the works devoted to German Catholicism, there are the collected texts in Father P. E. FICHTHAUT, *Deutsche Katholikentage 1848–1958 und soziale Frage* (Essen: Driemer, 1960, 409 pp.), and the rather exorbitant pamphlet by CARL AMERY, *Die Kapitulation, oder Deutscher Katholizismus heute* (Hamburg: Rowohlt, 1963, 126 pp.), while the Protestant E. MUELLER and Catholic B. HANSLLER, in *Klerikalisierung des offentlichen Lebens?* (Osnabrück:

Fromms Taschenbücher, 1963, 94 pp.), answer the question in their title in an emphatically negative way. A great deal of information on German Protestantism can be found in *Taschenbuch der evangelischen Kirchen in Deutschland 1962* (Stuttgart: Evangelisches Verlagswerk, 1962, 898 pp.).

Two postwar leaders of the Evangelical Church are presented, one by an uncritical admirer, the other by himself, in DIETMAR SCHMIDT, *Pastor Niemöller* (London: Odhams Press, 1959, 224 pp.), and OTTO DIBELIUS, *Eir Christ ist immer im Dienst: Erlebnisse und Erfahrungen in einer Zeitwende* (Stuttgart: Kreuz Verlag, 1961, 340 pp.). EBERHARD STAMMLER provides the most intelligently critical portrait of contemporary German Protestantism in *Protestanten ohne Kirche* (Stuttgart: Kreuz Verlag, 1960, 231 pp.).

On the problems of German youth, there is the excellent monthly published in Munich called *Deutsche Jugend*. Among many available recent books on the same topic, HERMANN BERTLEIN, *Das Selbstverständnis der Jugend heute* (Darmstadt: Schröbel, 1960, 348 pp.), and WALTER JAIDE, *Eine neue Generation?* (Munich: Juventa, 1960, 190 pp.) are noteworthy, but students of German affairs must still depend on the revealing and thoughtful interviews and analyses in G. WURZBACHER, et al., *Die junge Arbeiterin* (Munich: Juventa, 1958, 454 pp.).

Student life in Germany is, of course, an issue in itself, one that is examined in an albeit inconclusive fashion by JÜRGEN HABERMAS in *Student und Politik* (Neuwied: Luchterhand, 1961, 359 pp.); two other studies of the student corporations are, perhaps, better—one that is favorable to them, BERNARD OUDIN, *Les Corporations allemandes*

d'étudiants (Paris: Librairie générale de droit et de jurisprudence, 1962, 165 pp.), and one that is very critical and
much better informed, LUTZ FINKE, *Gestatte mir Hoch-
achtungsschluck: Bundesdeutschlands korporative Elite*
(Hamburg: Rütten & Löning, 1963, 168 pp.). The issues of
reform in the universities and the democratization of education are debated by HELMUT SCHELSKY in *Einsamkeit und
Freiheit: Idee und Gestalt der deutschen Universität und
ihre Reformen* (Hamburg: Rowohlt, 1963, 342 pp.), and,
more important, by HELMUT BECKER in *Quantität und
Qualität: Grundfragen der Bildungspolitik* (Freiburg:
Rombach, 1962, 416 pp.).

What is the role of the intellectual in contemporary German society? In *Die Intellektuellen: Wirkung, Versagen,
Verdienst* (Munich: Olzog, 1961, 104 pp.), PAUL NOACK
offers a succinct but pertinent answer. Attacks against the
embourgeoisement and satiety of German society constitute
one important facet of the intellectuals' function, in any
case, and they do not spare themselves in this regard—see,
for instance, GERHARD ZWERENZ, *Aergernisse: Von der
Maas bis an die Memel* (Cologne: Kiepenheuer & Witsch,
1961, 341 pp.) and *Wider die deutschen Tabus* (Munich:
List, 1962, 191 pp.), but above all, the volume edited by
HANS WERNER RICHTER, the man who inspired the Group
47, *Bestandaufnahme: Eine deutsche Bilanz 1962* (Munich:
Desch, 1962, 592 pp.). See also *Almanach der Gruppe 47,
1957–1962* (Hamburg: Rowohlt, 1962, 469 pp.), also
edited by Richter.

It is difficult to say, of course, to what degree the positive
and negative elements in a society balance out. The excellent analysis by W. HARTENSTEIN and G. SCHUBERT,
Mitlaufen oder Mitbestimmen (Frankfort: Europäische

Verlagsanstalt, 1961, 103 pp.), emphasizes the conformist
intolerance in German society. To get a more precise image
of the ideology of the Federal Republic, there is also PETER
SCHOENBACH, *Reaktionen auf die antisemitische Welle im
Winter 1959–1960* (Frankfort: Europäische Verlagsanstalt,
1960, 104 pp.); H. VAN DAM, RALPH GIORDANO, eds.,
KZ-Verbrecher vor deutschen Gerichten (Frankfort:
Europäische Verlagsanstalt, 1962, 583 pp.); and KARL
MIELCKE, *1917–1945 in den Geschictsbüchern der Bundesrepublik* (Hanover: Niedersächsische Landeszentrale für
politische Bildung, 1961, 165 pp.).

The Federal Republic in International Life

German works on this topic in general lack objectivity;
even the most serious studies do not examine the various
divergent themes in any depth. One can, however, recommend the following three books: GERHARD SCHEUNER, *Die
Rechtslage des geteilten Deutschland* (Frankfort: Metzner,
1960, 175 pp.); RUDOLPH SCHUSTER, *Deutschlands staatliche
Existenz im Widerstreit politischer und rechtlicher
Gesichtspunkte, 1945–1963* (Munich: Oldenbourg, 1963,
308 pp.); and DIETER RAUSCHNING, ed., *Die Gesamtver-
fassung Deutschlands: Nationale und internationale Texte
zur Rechtslage Deutschlands* (Frankfort: Metzner, 1962,
798 pp.). For a concise presentation of an SPD view that
is almost entirely acceptable to the CDU, there is ADOLF
ARNDT, *Der deutsche Staat als Rechtsproblem* (Berlin: de
Gruyter, 1960, 48 pp.).

There is no good general work on German foreign policy
since 1949, although there is RÜDIGER ALTMANN's brilliant
essay *Das deutsche Risiko: Aussenpolitische Perspektiven*

(Stuttgart: Seewald, 1962, 146 pp.). See also ALFRED
GROSSER, "France and Germany in the Atlantic Commu-
nity," in FRANCIS WILCOX and H. FIELD HAVILAND, eds.,
The Atlantic Community (New York: Praeger, 1963, pp.
32–55). The collected speeches and articles by two leading
German figures in the field are interesting: the first is by
the late HEINRICH VON BRENTANO, *Germany and Europe:
Reflections on German Foreign Policy;* Foreword by LUD-
WIG ERHARD (New York: Frederick A. Praeger; London:
André Deutsch, 1964); and the second is by WILHELM
GREWE, *Deutsche Aussenpolitik der Nachkriegszeit* (Stutt-
gart: Deutsche Verlagsanstalt, 1960, 539 pp.). There is also
KARL DEUTSCH and LEWIS EDINGER, *Germany Rejoins the
Powers: Mass Opinion, Interest Groups, and Elites in
Contemporary German Foreign Policy* (Stanford: Stan-
ford University Press, 1959, 320 pp.), and HANS SPEIER
and W. PHILLIPS DAVISON, *West German Leadership and
Foreign Policy* (Evanston and New York: Harper & Row,
1957).

The book by NORBERT TÖNNIS, *Der Weg zu den
Waffen: Die Geschichte der deutschen Wiederbewaffnung,
1959–1961* (Rastatt: Pabel, 1961, 156 pp.), is rather too
close to the official line on the subject, but it is a good
chronological study of German postwar rearmament, which
is well complemented by HANS SPEIER, *German Rearmament and Atomic War: The Views of German Military and
Political Leaders* (Evanston and New York: Harper &
Row, 1957, 272 pp.). For a more recent discussion of stra-
tegic concepts and problems, there is HELMUT SCHMIDT,
trans., Edward Thomas, *Defense or Retaliation: A German
View* (New York: Praeger, 1962, 264 pp.), and FRITZ
ERLER and RICHARD JAEGER, *Sicherheit und Rüstung* (Co-

logne: Verlag für Wissenschaft und Politik, 1962, 187 pp.).

A thorough discussion of Franco-German relations, as well as a good bibliography on the subject, is provided in the volumes of the German-French Institute in Ludwigsburg, *Deutschland-Frankreich* (Stuttgart: Deutsche Verlagsanstalt, 1954, 378 pp.; 1957, 472 pp.; and 1963, 288 pp.). The issue of the Saar is covered in the excellent book by JACQUES FREYMOND, *The Saar Conflict, 1945–1955* (New York: Praeger; London: Stevens, 1960, 423 pp.), and in the three well informed volumes of ROBERT H. SCHMIDT, *Saarpolitik, 1945–1957* (Berlin: Duncker & Humblot, 1959–62, 652, 784, 899 pp.).

Among the many books on Berlin, there are several worth mentioning: *Dokumente zur Berlin–Frage 1944–1962* (Munich: Oldenbourg, 2nd ed., 1962, 623 pp.); ELMAR PLISCHKE, *Government and Politics of Contemporary Berlin* (The Hague: Nijhoff, 1963, 119 pp.); SIEGFRIED MAMPEL's precise and thoughtful study, *Der Sowjetsektor von Berlin: Eine Analyse seines äusseren und inneren Status* (Frankfort: Metzner, 1963, 496 pp.); KURT PRITZKOLEIT, *Berlin: Ein Kampf uns Leben* (Düsseldorf, 1962, 179 pp.), a book that is at once more profound and more frank than those by other German authors; an interesting collection of German articles, CHARLES B. ROBSON, ed., *Berlin: Pivot of German Destiny* (Chapel Hill: University of North Carolina Press, 1960, 233 pp.); DEANE and DAVID HELLER, *The Berlin Wall* (New York: Walker, 1962, 242 pp.), a good book that nevertheless will not replace H. W. RICHTER, ed., *Die Mauer oder der 13 August* (Hamburg: Rowohlt, 1961, 196 pp.). JEAN SCHWOEBEL's informative *Les deux K, Berlin, et la paix* (Paris: Julliard, 1963, 329 pp.) is considerably more critical of German politics than the other books listed here.

The Oder-Neisse line and relations with Poland are rarely examined objectively or serenely. A courageous and intelligent book by GEORG BLUHM, *Die Oder-Neisse Linie in der deutschen Aussenpolitik* (Freiburg: Rombach, 1963, 204 pp.), is the exception. ZOLTAN M. SZAZ, *Germany's Eastern Frontiers: The Problem of the Oder-Neisse Line* (Chicago: Regnery, 1960, 256 pp.), is one-sided. ELIZABETH WISKE-MANN's aggressive but very useful study, *Germany's Eastern Neighbours* (London, New York: Oxford University Press, 1956, 309 pp.), has become the center of a violent controversy in Germany itself. But is a German-Polish dialogue in itself a decoy? The collected pieces in *Heimatrecht in polnischer und deutscher Sicht* (Leer, Ostfriesland: Rautenberg, 1962, 127 pp.) present various irreconcilable views. But a book like HANSJAKOB STEHLE's *The Independent Satellite: Society and Politics in Poland Since 1945* (New York: Frederick A. Praeger; London: Pall Mall, 1965) shows a change in the climate of opinion, nevertheless. Lastly, there is KARL JASPER's stimulating work, to read whether one agrees or criticizes, *Freiheit und Wiedervereinigung: Über Aufgaben deutscher Politik* (Munich: Piper, 1960, 123 pp.).

Index